THROUGH THE
OPEN DOOR

Through
THE
Open Door

A NEW LOOK AT
C. S. LEWIS

DABNEY ADAMS HART

THE UNIVERSITY OF ALABAMA PRESS

Library of Congress Cataloging in Publication Data

Hart, Dabney Adams, 1926–
   Through the open door.

   Bibliography: p.
   Includes index.
   1. Lewis, C. S. (Clive Staples), 1898–1963—Criticism
and interpretation. I. Title.
PR6023.E926Z673   1984   828'.91209   83-6520
   ISBN 0-8173-0187-9

91328

CONTENTS

PREFACE

The splendid irony of C. S. Lewis's reputation and influence is that this conservative Christian medievalist encouraged radical reassessments in all his writing. One of his favorite images was the open door: the opportunity for new perspectives, new views, free movement of the mind and spirit. The purpose of this book is to show how this theme unifies and dominates Lewis's varied works.

Though the key to my interpretation was given me by Lewis himself when we met in 1956, I did not try the lock until recent years. I have been inspired to share my ideas by the response of numerous audiences who have asked me to talk and teach about Lewis. In addition to these people of all ages and types, many individuals have been helpful in opening doors. My colleague Hugh Keenan, who suggested that I submit a paper on Lewis for a conference, got me started; my department chairman, Paul Blount, who allowed me released time, enabled me to finish. The encouragement of Clyde S. Kilby, now retired as curator of the Marion E. Wade Collection at Wheaton College, gave me confidence; and the friendship of Caroline Rakestraw, now retired as director of the Episcopal Radio TV Foundation, sustained my determination to get the book written.

Elizabeth McWhorter, Mary Anderson, and Georgia Christopher read the manuscript in various drafts and made excellent suggestions. Although I have done most of the typing myself, Brenda Coker's help at a crucial stage was invaluable.

My indebtedness and appreciation go back to much earlier stages. I would never have been able to write this book without research in London, under the benevolent guidance of Professor John Crow at King's College, and I would never have started the project without the cooperation of Professor Paul Wiley of the University of Wisconsin. My longest-standing gratitude is to my mother, who introduced me to Lewis when I was in my impressionable teens and is still helping me by proofreading.

THROUGH THE
OPEN DOOR

Chapter I

FACE TO FACE
WITH C. S. LEWIS

*" . . . how would it be if you came and
had tea with me?"* —THE LION, THE
WITCH AND THE WARDROBE

When I was in graduate school at the University of
Wisconsin in the early 1950s, C. S. Lewis's *English Literature in the Sixteenth Century* joined *The Allegory of Love* and
A Preface to Paradise Lost as landmark scholarly criticism
for English majors. Some of my friends were also familiar with *The Screwtape Letters* as a classic of collegiate
religious discussion groups, and a few of us had read the
space trilogy. When I realized that the same Lewis had
written these varied books and was currently publishing
a series of children's tales, my search for a dissertation
topic suddenly came into focus. Instead of boring into
some as yet unscratched corner of a well-known writer's
corpus, I wanted to estimate the literary significance of a
writer whose work had never been considered as a
whole. In Lewis's writing I detected but could not describe a pattern in the grain.

The Wisconsin English faculty were reluctant to accept a proposal for a dissertation on the literary theory of
C. S. Lewis. Scholars in the Modern British field, where
he belonged as a living writer, did not consider him a
major creative talent and did not share his medieval and

Renaissance interests. But Professor Paul Wiley was generous-spirited enough to agree to direct my farfetched intentions, and the Fulbright Committee backed me with a scholarship for research in England. In 1955 very little had been written about Lewis. Chad Walsh's *Apostle to the Skeptics*[1] had treated religious themes, but the only assessments of his literary achievements were in reviews of individual books. Much of Lewis's own criticism was in periodicals and monographs not available in the United States. I needed a year in England to prove to myself as well as to my committee that my topic was important.

In 1954 Lewis had startled English academic circles with his inaugural address as Professor of Medieval and Renaissance Literature in the University of Cambridge. Describing the two periods thus united in his new chair as closely related phases of "Old Western culture," Lewis postulated that changes in politics, the arts, religion, and technology have caused a greater divide within the past century than at any other period in history. Between the time of Sir Walter Scott or Jane Austen and the second half of the twentieth century, "a new archetypal image . . . of old machines being superseded by new and better ones" has been imposed on the human mind.[2] Identifying himself as an Old Western man rather than a modern, Lewis claimed a special qualification for his new job: "You don't want to be lectured on Neanderthal Man by a Neanderthaler, still less on dinosaurs by a dinosaur. And yet, is that the whole story? If a live dinosaur dragged its slow length into the laboratory, would we not all look back as we fled? . . . I would give a great deal to hear any Athenian, even a stupid one, talking about Greek tragedy. He would know in his bones so much that we seek in vain. . . . where I fail as a critic, I may yet be useful as a specimen. . . . use your specimens while you can. There are not going to be many more dinosaurs."[3] When

Lewis's *Surprised By Joy* and the third volume of Tolkien's *The Lord of the Rings* were published in the fall of 1955, both these Old Western men became increasingly popular. The dinosaur image seemed inappropriate, but none of the reviews anticipated the influence Lewis and Tolkien would have on the next generation.

Soon I had an opportunity to see and hear the "specimen" when he gave a series of four lectures at Oxford, his first official return engagement as a Cambridge professor. He had been at "the other university" for more than a year but spent weekends and vacations at his home just outside Oxford. Therefore the lectures were scheduled for his convenience at five o'clock on Friday afternoon and ten-thirty Saturday morning on two consecutive November weekends. I was amazed when a Rhodes scholar friend insisted that we should have tea early at a shop in the High, across the street from the lecture hall, in order to get good seats; but he was right: by five o'clock people were standing. When Lewis began to speak it was obvious why he could attract hundreds of students and faculty to hear about Milton's minor poems, as many on the second Saturday as on the first Friday.

Lewis was a consummate entertainer, illustrating Milton's artistry with some of the techniques he ascribed to Milton. He called the Latin elegies "poetry at the lowest level—on a par with the joiner's art or fencing." The fifth in particular, he thought, must have been more fun to write than to read. The image of the graceful flourish, parry, and thrust depicts Lewis's own style. He obviously had fun sharing his views on Milton, just as he said Milton in "L'Allegro" and "Il Penseroso" was expressing nothing more than the enjoyment of making the poems. He was the "old Mozartian Milton," using poetry as now only music is used for occasions and moods. His artistry could even be described in a culinary metaphor: Lewis urged us to think of *Comus* as a "confection, in which Platonic theology, etc., are the ingredients. The art is the *blend*." But Lewis's flourishes were accompanied by rapier thrusts at critics who misjudge the minor poems by taking them more seriously than Milton intended. Lewis said, for instance, that *Comus* could not be elucidated by an anthropologist's study of savage rites and taboos, since Milton was neither an anthropologist nor a savage. The best critic of *Samson Agonistes* would be a man in a concentration camp confronted with a glamorous spy.

This random sampling of my notes may give some impression of Lewis's charm as a lecturer. I recognized some characteristic themes and stylistic features of his criticism, but there was one unexpected element that I did not fully appreciate until much later. On the last morning Lewis began with a gracious retraction of a comment the afternoon before about Aristotle: that he had ignored the Dionysian elements in tragedy. Conversation in the evening with a better Aristotelian than himself led him to agree that possibly Aristotle had merely thought it unnecessary to mention what everyone took for granted. Lewis's careful attention to this correction struck me as significant for Lewis as much as for Aristotle and *Samson Agonistes*. He was showing how easy it is to make a mistake, how likely one is to be wrong. With all his genial assurance about the right way to enjoy Milton, Lewis was never authoritarian. Yet the more I learned about him and his work, the more convinced I became of his authoritative consistency.

After an academic year of research on the literary theory underlying all of Lewis's work, I convinced my London University faculty adviser that my bibliography was reasonably comprehensive. He sent it to Lewis, asking him to check it for possible omissions and indicating that its compiler would welcome an interview. The reply was characteristically prompt, concise, helpful, and generous.

28/5/56

Dear Mr. Crow

I return Miss Adams' list with a few *addenda*. I can't remember anything else which she has omitted; and if I don't, it's not likely anyone else will. If the lady really thinks it worth her while to come & see an author who is no v. accurate scholar in his own works, of course she is welcome to do so. I shall be here till June 8th, after that at The Kilns, Headington Quarry, Oxford.

Yours sincerely

C. S. Lewis

On a separate page there were five items: an introduction in an anthology, three articles in *Theology,* and an unsigned review. He noted that he had forgotten a few other short reviews, and on the back of the envelope he added a P.S. about "some things in *The Month.*"

My elation at this response was tempered, though not diminished, by the subtlety of Lewis's self-deprecation. He took neither himself nor my research very seriously. He had recently expressed his low estimation of the American Ph.D. system in a *Cambridge Review* article comparing Oxford and Cambridge (reluctantly, and only under pressure from the student editors):

The other evil (on my view) is the incubus of "Research." The system was, I believe, first devised to attract the Americans and to emulate the scientists. But the wisest Americans are themselves already sick of it. . . . it is surely clear by now that the needs of the humanities are different from those of the scientists. . . . the man who has just got his First in English or Modern Languages, . . . far from being able or anxious . . . to add to the sum of human knowledge, wants to acquire a good deal more of the knowledge we already have. . . . What keeps the system going is the fact that it becomes increasingly difficult to get an academic job without a "research degree."[4]

Lewis would have considered it more worth the lady's while to read Greats at Oxford or to immerse herself in medieval literature than to write a dissertation on him.

Despite this attitude, he was gracious in his reply to my letter leaving the decision about place and date to him:

1/6/56

Dear Miss Adams

I think it wd. be more use to you to come here, for it is here that I have two fat envelopes full of old articles etc. which you cd. go through to see if you've missed anything (wh. you most likely have *not*). I have two sitting rooms, so you can have one to yourself and do the job in peace and comfort. Wednesday wd. be the best day. Shall I expect you at about 2 o'clock?

Yours sincerely
C. S. Lewis

When I arrived at Lewis's set of rooms in Magdalene College, I was beginning to wonder why I had come, how I dared intrude. Lewis had always stressed that what the writer intends should be clear in what he writes. To raise questions about meaning would indicate either his failure or my stupidity; to raise questions about himself would represent what he disparaged as "the personal heresy."

The minute Lewis opened the door, looking exactly like one of the genially smiling pictures on the book covers, he put me completely at ease. The only features of his comfortable, nondescript, somewhat cluttered living room that I remember are the big sofa opposite the fireplace and the long, low coffee table where I could spread out the scribbled notes, incomplete drafts of poems, offprints of articles, and newspaper clippings that he offered me to look through. Also on the table was a gift box of chocolates that he urged me to finish up since he was "supposed to be slimming." I felt as if I were visiting a favorite uncle. I realize now that Lewis was like the thoughtful adult in a childless household who provides a box of toys or curios for young visitors. Most of the newspaper articles I had seen; some of the fragments were intriguing. The material did not seem significant, and I gathered that Lewis himself did not know or care what was there.

My attention was distracted only once in two hours, when Lewis answered a knock at the door. A young man's voice said eagerly, "Professor Lewis, the chalice has just come and I wanted you to be the first to see it." They crossed behind the sofa and went into the study without disturbing me, so I glimpsed nothing but a brown paper package. Presumably the new chalice was for the college chapel; obviously the new professor's door was always open to students.

My host took it for granted that his American visitor would stay for tea. He boiled the water in an electric kettle on the hearth, made the tea in a plain earthenware pot, and served some delectable cream-filled pastries bought at the bakery especially for me. Thus fortified in traditional English fashion, we talked about how Americans regard English literature. Lewis said he had always marveled that people who had never seen the hedgerows and sheepfolds of the English countryside could understand the imagery of English poetry. He was sorry that I had not read Robert Penn Warren's *Band of Angels,* which had interested him as a male novelist's use of a female narrator. Instead of talking about his work, he asked me about my year in England and my teaching in the United States. I did not know that he had recently married an American and did not mention that I had become engaged to an Englishman. His warm and sensitive response to a new acquaintance was focused on our mutual interests in literature and teaching.

The closest Lewis came to a personal remark was some gentle teasing about my scholarly pursuits. As I was leaving, he advised: "You had better finish your dissertation promptly before I publish something that will invalidate your conclusions." Thus finally, on the doorstep, he challenged me to ask, "What do you mean?" But it was too late for questions. I had already said that I must catch the next train to London, and I did not want to overstay my welcome.

At the time, I interpreted Lewis's parting shot as a joke. He fulfilled the avuncular role with tongue in cheek and discharged the professional duty of prodding a student into action. He warned me not so much about what he might do as about what I had done already. I inferred that his low estimation of the value of graduate research in the humanities included mine, whatever I might have revealed about his work. He was not interested enough in himself as a writer to care about my conclusions, which I thought were more perceptive and comprehensive than he would have expected. I could not believe that he would ever publish anything inconsistent with the doctrine of mythopoeia, which was my focus.

When Lewis's *Till We Have Faces* came out later in 1956, I realized that his comment about Warren's woman narrator referred to this fourth experiment with the novel as a form. His use of the Cupid and Psyche myth was very different from the Ransom trilogy, but there was no challenge to my major premise that Lewis's idea about the function of myth in the human imagination was the heart and core of all his writing in every form. I became convinced that Lewis had been poking fun at the very idea of himself as a dissertation subject.

He did, however, have some surprises up his sleeve. In a 1958 article in the *Christian Herald,* "Will We Lose God in Outer Space?"[5] Lewis proposed that space travel might challenge the basic Christian tenet of man's uniqueness. There could be rational species for whom Christ's incarnation and sacrifice would be irrelevant. God would have made a different Covenant with them. This intriguing idea attracted the attention of *Time* and inspired a typical caption for the picture of a balding, smiling, relaxed professor: "Explorer Lewis / Beyond gravity, no fall?"[6] Whatever the theologians made of Lewis's speculations, the connection with his novels and children's stories was clear. The nonhuman rational and spiritual creatures in his fiction, profoundly true as images, might prove closer to fact than he or his readers had imagined. However surprising the *Christian Herald* article may have been for some readers of Lewis's religious works, any who had understood his novels recognized a similar theme.

Every book or article published during Lewis's lifetime confirmed my conclusions. Since his death in 1963, new material has continued to appear. His literary executor has edited previously unpublished material, brought out collections of articles from diverse and inaccessible sources, and edited one group of letters. Lewis's brother edited the first collection of letters, and many more have been made available to readers in the Bodleian Library at Oxford and the Wade Collection at Wheaton College in Illinois. Critical studies have proliferated so rapidly that the twelve-page bibliography included in a 1969 book[7] was superseded in 1974 by a 353-page bibliographical volume.[8] Now a lengthy supplement would be required to bring the list up to date. In all this attention to Lewis—primarily in the United States—he has been recognized as a master mythmaker.

During the twenty years I lived in England, while most of the children I knew read the *Chronicles of Narnia* and my Christian friends were familiar with *Screwtape*, no one ever asked me to give a talk or paper on Lewis. The prophet was by no means without honor in his own country, particularly among those of my friends who had read English at Oxford, but there were no seminars, no study groups at churches, no conferences (I did not then realize the extent of these activities in the United States). In the early 1970s I was surprised to get a letter from a nun in a convent college in India, asking if I could send her a copy of my dissertation. In her study of Lewis she had learned that it was available on microfilm, but she was hundreds of miles from the nearest microfilm reader. I mailed a typescript that took months to reach her and years to get back to me. I thought she might be my only reader.

When I came back to the United States in 1975, I soon discovered that C. S. Lewis's popularity had continued to increase. Negotiations for the television production of *The Lion, the Witch and the Wardrobe* were in progress, church groups wanted to hear about Lewis from someone who had met him, colleges were offering seminars on the Inklings, and professional conferences welcomed papers on his work. I gradually realized that in studying the dinosaur I had been avant-garde. My dissertation on Lewis was the first; what I did not find out until 1979 was that it had been available in a printout at the Wade Collection and recommended as a starting point for

Lewis students for nearly twenty years. When I finally had an opportunity to visit Wheaton College for a conference, I met people who recognized my name as a pioneer of Lewis studies. Many of them wondered why I had never published.

This book is the answer to that question. Although Lewis never invalidated my original conclusions, his warning was prophetic. Much of what I said about him in the late 1950s is still valid but irrelevant in the early 1980s. He does not need my defense; his reputation and influence far exceed my predictions. Although he did not change his views, my perception of his significance has been reshaped. I now see the theory of mythopoeia not only as the basis of all Lewis's fiction and criticism, but also as the perspective for his revisionary outlook.

In calling himself an Old Western man, a member of a dying species, Lewis affirmed his devotion to the culture whose decline grieved him. But his choice of image is significant. The dinosaur was not the supreme achievement of the Creator. Old forms may be superseded, for better or worse. The most carefully calculated conclusions or deeply entrenched convictions may be invalidated by new revelation. Lewis always stressed that he was elucidating a subject in the light of his present understanding. The undercurrent throughout is reminiscent of St. Paul: "For now we see through a glass darkly, but then face to face." This is the lesson that Lewis had been teaching all along.

Chapter II

MYTH:

THE MASTER KEY

It is the myth that gives life.—GOD IN
THE DOCK

When C. S. Lewis recommended that his Cambridge students regard their new Professor of Medieval and Renaissance Literature as a laboratory specimen, he was directing their attention not to himself but to an image of what he called "Old Western" man. He urged them to study a practicing Christian with his Hebraic and Hellenic background as an almost obsolete species. Yet Lewis was actually avant-garde as a critic: he stressed the primacy of myth in literature before Joseph Campbell, Mircea Eliade, and Northrop Frye had established their reputations in that field. In 1939 Lewis wrote that he would not expect a contributor to the *Times Literary Supplement* to understand "the esoteric doctrine of myths."[1] The concept of mythopoeia has now become widely familiar to readers as well as reviewers of serious contemporary literature; it is the starting point for perceiving the unity within the diversity of C. S. Lewis's work.

One aspect of Lewis's diversity is the range in his use of the term *myth.* In common parlance, *myth* is often used as an antonym of *fact, truth,* or *history.* When some evidence of petrified gopher wood is found on Mount Ararat, or digging in southwest England uncovers what could be the site of Camelot, there is excitement about the possibility of confirming a beloved myth. For Lewis, in contrast, the best evidence of truth was the myth's universal popularity. He affirmed, in all his writing in all genres, that myth is an expression of universal truth in terms that the human imagination can apprehend.

Myth is, basically, any kind of story that succeeds in transcending the laws of mathematics, the whole being greater than the sum of its parts. The stories of the dying and reviving god, the search for the visionary mistress or the Holy Grail, the experience of Cinderella, Prometheus, or Hamlet are examples (cited by Lewis in various contexts) of some of the great myths of our civilization. Whether they have any basis in fact is irrelevant, for the *fact* is that they are stories that live in themselves. Their power depends on their recreation of universal human experience: they are recognizably true to life. But because they seem at the same time more true than any one person's particular experience of life, they suggest that this power derives ultimately from universal truth itself. According to Lewis, "the value of myth is that it takes all the things we know and restores to them the rich significance which has been hidden by 'the veil of familiarity.'"[2] Myth is a story of what *happens* as distinguished from, but not contradictory to, the history of what *has happened*. The relationship between myth and history is complementary, in that each is a human vision of events forming a pattern. The patterns of myth are more universal than those of history, their appeal on a deeper level.

Lewis accepted as an act of faith the Christian doctrines in which myth and history are united: incarnation, sacrifice, resurrection, and atonement. The story of his conversion from agnosticism to theism and thence to

Christianity, as told by Lewis himself and by others, began when his imagination was "baptized" at sixteen by the appeal of a fantasy bought casually to read on the train. He often acknowledged his lifelong debt to George MacDonald's *Phantastes,* particularly by making the Scottish preacher and storyteller his guide in the afterlife in *The Great Divorce.* The baptism of his imagination came long before his acceptance of dogma and was clearly distinguished from it. For the appreciation of literature, the imagination's response to myth is what matters. In discussing Shelley's version of the Prometheus story, Lewis said: "Like all great myths, its primary appeal is to the imagination: its indirect and further appeal to the will and the understanding can therefore be diversely interpreted according as the reader is a Christian, a politician, a psychoanalyst, or what not."[3] The relationship between the universal myth and any related doctrine is a philosophical question, as Lewis discussed in many sermons, lectures, and articles, such as those now collected in *God in the Dock.*[4]

The concept of myth as the basis of literature depends on Lewis's theory that allegory is inherent in the human imagination. He considered that the essence of thought and language is allegorical—the realization of the insensible in terms of the sensible. The immediate and operative links forged by the imagination between abstract and concrete make a meaningful chain; the folk bards who fashioned these chains into stories were the originators of literature. In his first major critical and historical study, *The Allegory of Love,* Lewis tried to explain medieval sensibility to the generally unsympathetic 1930s by claiming that allegory is the most psychologically natural of all literary forms, and that the difficult problem is not how the taste for it developed but rather how it deteriorated.[5] The solution to that problem, suggested throughout his critical and imaginative writing, is stated explicitly in the introduction to *English Literature in the Sixteenth Century*: the old mythical imagination, the birthright of humanity, has been lost by the increasing emphasis on the mathematical methodology of science.[6] Whatever the empirical values of or proofs for scientific modes of thought, Lewis insisted that the allegorical mode of the imagination is the natural one. Scientific thinking must be learned, superimposed on man's deepest instincts, which are the soundest guide to what is truly significant.

Lewis's claim for the instinctive imagination as the touchstone of reality was based on his experience of response to truth in myth. But the conviction that myth embodies universal truth depends on the validity of the imagination. Thus Lewis could be challenged, from the logician's point of view, for apparently begging the question. Indeed the whole idea of literature as mythmaking may be challenged as limited to nonrealistic fiction, including epics, romances, novels, and fantasies but excluding verse and prose of other genres. Lewis himself recognized the difficulties of his position. In *An Experiment in Criticism,* after an explanation of what he meant by myth, he acknowledged that its place in literature is not essential nor its appeal universal. "I have met literary people who had no taste for myth, but I have never met an unliterary person who had it."[7] The implication seems clear that while Lewis obviously included nonmythic writing in the canons of literature, he stressed mythic elements as primary in the literary experience of most human beings of all periods and cultures.

What Lewis consistently affirmed about the human imagination can perhaps be tested only by sharing what he called an "experience with a razor's edge which remakes the whole mind, which produces the 'holy spectral shiver.'"[8] His evidence is no more irrefutable proof than Wordsworth's "intimations" of immortality. Lewis tried always in his criticism to stimulate imagination rather than to force assent.

For the reader in sympathy with Lewis's idea of myth, its relationship to literature is consistent. Myth is usually story, not just any unified sequence of events but a pattern of such powerful appeal to the imagination that it seems to have an existence of its own. The factor of plot is secondary, sometimes unnecessary. Lewis referred to "Natural Man," the idealization of the noble savage uncontaminated by civilization, as one of the great myths, and the only respect in which the exploration of America stimulated the imagination of the sixteenth century.[9] In this context *myth* seems to be synonymous with *image,* perhaps best understood as an embryonic myth with the potential of developing into mature story.

The myth's embodiment of human experience in literature takes different forms. Often an existing myth provides structure for a work of literature. In medieval poems and romances, the hero's search for the Holy Grail provides an imaginative center or framework for chronicle and moralizing. Spenser's combination of familiar myths in *The Faerie Queene,* O'Neill's American version of the *Oresteia,* or Lewis's own adaptation of the Cupid and Psyche story in *Till We Have Faces* are examples of myths used structurally. However, according to Lewis, even more powerful in the English tradition than explicit use of the mythology of Olympus or Camelot is the popular mythology of elves, dragons, and figures like Jack the Giant-Killer.

Although *myth* is usually interpreted as age-old story, Lewis often referred to new myths. A story like Orwell's *Animal Farm* is not simply a satiric allegory of the abuses of Soviet Communism; rather, it is a story that transcends its allegorical significance and becomes a full-fledged myth that speaks for itself.[10] It is an example of a story in which ". . . allegory rises to myth, in which the symbols, though fashioned to represent mere single concepts, take on new life and represent rather the principles—not otherwise accessible—which unite whole classes of concepts."[11] For instance, in the motto of the ruling class of pigs, "ALL ANIMALS ARE EQUAL BUT SOME ARE MORE EQUAL THAN OTHERS," the satire aimed at the Communist elite is overshadowed by the manifold significance of the capsule myth. Other familiar new myths include such Lewis favorites as *Pilgrim's Progress* and *Gulliver's Travels, The Time Machine* and *The Well at the World's End.* The next generation would add *The Old Man and the Sea* and *Lord of the Flies* to the list.

What makes a story myth, as opposed to allegory, is that there are "no specific pointers," as Lewis said in classifying Tolkien's *The Lord of the Rings* when he reviewed the first volume. Tolkien's story is not like Bunyan's. In the pilgrim's adventures, each specific pointer—the narrow gate, the burden, the slough, or the river—equals an aspect of Christian experience; this is allegory that rises to myth. Tolkien, on the other hand, did not design his tale to represent aspects of a specific evil—Fascism, or industrialization, or any other power that some of the first critics thought they could identify; *The Lord of the Rings* is not allegory but myth. Emphasizing its difference from any conventional genres, Lewis affirmed that the myth creates both its own genre and its own meaning. Although its truth is universal, or perhaps *because* it is universal, it admits various interpretations. "A myth points, for each reader, to the realm he lives in most. It is a master key; use it on what door you like."[12] Whether the myth be an old one that gives structure to the work or a new one that creates its own form, the basis of narrative literature is mythmaking, mythopoeia. It is not literary art that gives power to myth, but myth that charges literature with its vitality.

His concept of the supremacy of myth led Lewis to some unusual but consistent conclusions. In evaluating his beloved George MacDonald, the nineteenth-century writer of romances, he acknowledged that his style was never quite successful, a defect that barred him from the first ranks but not from the company of the great poets.[13] The poet, in the Greek sense of maker or creator, is the writer whose imagination is informed by an "*Idea* which organizes and masters all the diverse experiences he is working on."[14] This *Idea* is not a message but a myth, as it functions in the poet's imagination. MacDonald succeeded in communicating his formative myths to his readers, although he sometimes used a literary form unsuited to his talents—his century's dominant form, the novel. His style is far more successful in his fairy tales. In either genre, style is secondary to the mythic core.

The literary genre or form is distinct from the essential form of a work as determined by the myth or *Idea*. Lewis's concept of the mythic form or *Idea* was Platonic, with emphasis on the universality of the form or *Logos*. The most successful writers, in his view, are those whose mythopoetic forms are most compatible with the literary form that they choose. Both Sir Walter Scott and Jane Austen, for instance, found the novel to be the perfect embodiment of their formative *Ideas*. Lewis defined the novel in terms not of its "comment on life" but of its derivation from both tragedy and comedy:

Both were deliberate patterns or arrangements of possible (but by no means necessarily probable) events chosen for their harmonious unity in variety, deliberately modified, contrasted, balanced in a fashion which real life never permits. Different degrees of verisimilitude occur in different pieces, but I think the verisimilitude is always a means not an end. Improbability is avoided, when at all, not because the author wants to tell us what life is like, but because he fears lest too gross an improbability should make the audience incredulous and therefore unreceptive of the mood or passion he is trying to evoke.[15]

Lewis found in Scott no specific theme or message, but a story told with a sound and moral sense of proportion. Jane Austen, in contrast, united story and message. The basic structure underlying her four most characteristic novels is the theme of "undeception" in moral terms; this theme intensified the "harmonious unity in variety," creating a pattern similar to the central pattern of the comedy of Molière. Since her moral emphasis is on conduct, the balance and contrast of events in the novel form is the perfect expression for this thematic *Idea*.[16]

Literary genre is not sacrosanct, and neither George MacDonald nor George Orwell can be written off for his failure with the novel as a form. Whether *Animal Farm* or *1984* is a novel is irrelevant; the former is superior, in Lewis's estimation, because all of its matter is relevant to its subject, its "animals" are deeply human, and its myth creates its own form.[17] Similarly, More's *Utopia,* which has been called a comic satire and a philosophical treatise, transcends controversy over its genre, and achieves its status as a classic, through the mythic power of its imaginary geography, politics, economics, and sociology.[18] Even the great form of tragedy is incidental to the Hamlet myth. In a characteristically provocative lecture called "Hamlet: The Prince or the Poem?" Lewis suggested that the disagreement among critics about the character of

Hamlet may come from a misguided attempt to judge *Hamlet* by the canons of formal tragedy; perhaps the pleasure of the play is not from character delineation of a tragic hero but from the mythopoetic creation of an enchanted world.[19]

This enchanted world, the myth itself, the literary *Idea,* is distinct not only from style and genre but also from the writer's own ideas—political, moral, religious, or philosophical. In contrasting the direct imaginative appeal of the myth in Shelley's *Prometheus Unbound* with the indirect philosophical interpretations, Lewis pointed out that the Christian interpretation is not necessarily the best from a literary perspective. However greatly the Christian possibilities of meaning may enhance the poem for some readers or detract for others, these religious ideas are subordinate to the magnificent structural *Idea* of Prometheus set at liberty. In such works as *Paradise Lost* or *Pilgrim's Progress,* the literary or poetic *Idea* does represent the author's religious ideas; whereas in *The Faerie Queene* or the plays of Shakespeare, the poetic *Idea* is constant and the philosophical ideas are dependent variables. Lewis insisted categorically: "I do not think Shakespeare wrote a single line to express 'his' ideas. . . . Spenser expected his readers to find . . . not his philosophy but their own experience—everyone's experience—loosened from its particular contexts by the universalizing power of allegory."[20] This distinction between *ideas* in the sense of opinions and *Idea* in the sense of myth is necessary to avoid irrelevant judgments, either of approval or of disapproval. The critic cannot prove or disprove that Chaucer was a Lollard or Spenser a Calvinist on the basis of their poetry, nor evaluate *Pilgrim's Progress* with reference to his own opinion about the Dissenters. Neither should he confuse his moral objections to certain kinds of sexual experience or violence in literature with objections of taste to triteness or pomposity.[21] Lewis's low estimation of D. H. Lawrence's fiction was, he insisted, based not on Lawrence's preoccupation with sex but on his undisciplined prose. His high regard for Charles Williams's novels might seem to indicate the bias of religion and friendship; but Lewis pointed out that he became acquainted with Williams through admiring his books rather than the other way round. Moreover, one of the twentieth-century writers he praised most often and most highly was H. G. Wells, mythmaker of *The Time Machine;* Lewis disapproved of Wells as an outspoken atheist and flaunter of conventional sexual morality, but he distinguished carefully between moral and aesthetic judgments.

Lewis's concept of the mythic basis of literature involves a controversial theory of the relationship between the artist and the work of art. In contrast to the premise that art is the expression of the artist's personality, conscious or unconscious, Lewis defined art as the artist's expression of something outside himself, some beauty or truth of which his art is an image. He referred to the artist in terms of an inventor, who imagines and then makes a thing new in itself but embodying elementary and universal principles and properties. For instance, Tolkien, in *The Lord of the Rings,* achieved the "utmost reach of invention"[22] in creating something that seems to be no longer his but an independent entity. While the work of art is independent, indeed *because* it is independent, the artist himself is not; like the scientist or the inventor, he must subject himself and his imagination to the discipline of reality and truth. Obviously this analogy cannot be pressed too far: it is suggestive rather than demonstrative. In another context Lewis chose a biological analogy to describe the process of literary creation as artistic inspiration without intellectual control:

There is a stage in the invention of any long story at which the outsider would see nothing but chaos. Numerous alternatives written, half-written, and unwritten (the latter possibly the most influential of all) ferment together. . . . the story is an organism: it goes on surreptitiously growing or decaying while your back is turned. If it decays, the resumption of work is like trying to coax to life an almost extinguished fire, or to recapture the confidence of a shy animal which you had only partially tamed at your last visit. But if (as is more probable) it grows, proliferates, "wantons in its prime," then you will come back to find it

> Changed like a garden in the heat of spring
> After an eight-days' absence.

Fertile chaos has obliterated the paths.[23]

Because Lewis recognized the subtlety and complexity of the creative process, being himself a creator as well as a critic, his idea of the writer's subordination to the force of the story, or myth, was not rigid. He acknowledged varying degrees of independence in inspiration. A medieval writer like Thomas Malory was not at all independent: the *Morte Darthur* was not "his" work but a formulation of traditional subject matter expressing, possibly without the author's awareness, the implicit ideas of his society.[24] Later writers were liberated from the demand to use traditional material and became more self-conscious about the values of their own societies. Yet the true poet did not become free to express *himself*; his scope was enlarged from the world of knowledge and experience to a world of deeper meaning with its own power on which the mythmaker was and still is dependent. The power of this other world is responsible for the sense of anguish, of exaltation, and, above all, of what Lewis called "diuturnity" in Tolkien's fantasy. He summed up this view in a rhetorical question: "Is mythopoeia, after all, not the most, but the least, subjective of activities?"[25]

The affirmative response is in the classical tradition. Plato taught that the maker of any artifact was imitating its ideal form; Aristotle pointed out that the dramatist imitated the realities of human experience. For Lewis this wisdom of the Greeks was fulfilled in Christianity. Both the operation of grace and the process of revelation represent in religious terms what happens to the writer: he does not engage in spontaneous creation, as many modern critics assume; instead, he receives power and vision from the Creator and is thus enabled "to embody in terms of his own art some reflection of eternal Beauty and Wisdom."[26]

This assumption does not deny the artist's responsibility for and control over the terms of his own art. However powerfully his imagination is inspired by myth, the successful embodiment of it depends on the writer's own ability, which Lewis defined as "the unifying faculty." He explained this concept in his analysis of why one of the most popular of medieval works, the *Roman de la Rose,* is no longer read, while *The Divine Comedy* is widely available in inexpensive editions throughout the western world:

> If it is said that they differ in merely technical power, I reply that technique itself is only one manifestation of the unifying faculty. The power which welds raw masses of experience into a whole is the same which, in a single phrase, elicits from the chaos of language the perfect words and the perfect syntactical device. Thus, in a sense, Jean lacked nothing which Dante had, except the power to coordinate. But that exception is fatal. Because of it, Dante remains a strong candidate for the supreme poetical honors of the world, while Jean de Meun is read

only by professional scholars, and not by very many of them.[27]

The process of coordination, involving selection and arrangement of words, incidents, characters, and ideas, seemed to Lewis to be a fully conscious, deliberate action. Although what distinguishes literature from mere writing is the mythopoetic factor, what distinguishes degrees of excellence in literature is the writer's application of the unifying faculty.

Lewis's theory of mythopoeia involves the relationship between the work of art and the audience as well as the artist. Since the impulse of the genuine work of art is not self-expression, its purpose is not release or satisfaction for the artist but pleasure for the reader. The emphasis throughout Lewis's criticism is on the quantity and, particularly, the quality of pleasure produced by the work of art; but his concept of the imaginative faculty allows instruction to be included in delight, since what delights the imagination most is myth that embodies universal truths. His confidence in the imaginative faculty of the reader, as well as of the writer, led him to insist that dullness is the worst sin of literature. Though *The Shepherd's Calendar* was written by the author of *The Faerie Queene*, Lewis made no attempt to defend it; whatever technical merits it may have are outweighed by the fact that he found it boring.[28] Conversely, no technical defects or theoretical inconsistencies can diminish the greatness of a literary work that stirs most readers' imaginations. In his attempt to solve the riddle of *Hamlet,* Lewis quoted T. S. Eliot's rebuke: "' . . . more people have thought *Hamlet* a work of art because they have found it interesting, than have found it interesting because it is a work of art.'"[29] For Lewis this distinction, disparaged by Eliot, was the whole point: the reader's genuine appreciation is preferable to any cult of cultural values.[30] This view is correlative with, though not dependent on, a Christian concept: Unless you become as a little child you cannot enter the Kingdom of Heaven. Lewis attempted to clarify the point by saying: "You must not think I am setting up as a sort of literary Peter Pan who does not grow up. On the contrary, I claim that only those adults who have retained, with whatever additions and enrichments, their first childish response to poetry unimpaired, can be said to have grown up at all."[31]

Lewis never denied the importance of the additions and enrichments in literary appreciation. The acquisition of knowledge, the achievement of historical perspective, the accumulation of experience, and the conditioning of mind and ear to subtleties of language and rhythm—all these additions form the discriminating faculty, which Lewis often referred to by the conventional term "taste." Although the untutored imagination responds instinctively to a genuine work of art, a cultivated taste may be required to distinguish between various ranks of art. Sometimes even bad art gives the same pleasure as good art because the naïve reader grasps what the author intended but failed to embody, or because the reader imagines for himself what is lacking.[32] Taste enables the reader to recognize not what could have been but what actually is embodied in the work of art.

Since taste, unlike imagination, is acquired rather than innate, it is relative to time and circumstances. Separating the literature of one period and the reader of another are mutations in taste that must be comprehended and discounted before full enjoyment becomes possible. Lewis found a good example in Chaucer's *Troilus and Criseyde*: fourteenth-century readers admired it as a stylized courtly romance, whereas contemporary readers praise it as a forerunner of the psychological novel.[33] Chaucer's poem transcends these variations, but the greatest pleasure comes to those readers who can reconstruct in their own minds the taste of the original audience. The reader's judgment is more significant if his taste has been developed through literary studies. Although the essence of the work of art, the myth, speaks to something inherent in the reader's imagination, its incidental features of genre, style, and ideas often demand elucidation and experience. Lewis himself, in the triple role of scholar, critic, and teacher, believed that "the true aim of literary studies is to lift the student out of his provincialism by making him the 'spectator,' if not of all, yet of much, 'time and existence.'"[34]

In helping the student to extend his range as a "spectator," Lewis continually warned that the cultivation of sensitive perception is not a virtue. He saw in much modern criticism the danger of elevating taste from a means of enjoyment to an end in itself. Such aestheticism leads to the assumption that what appeals to popular, uncultivated taste is *ipso facto* inferior. Because of his confidence in the inherent soundness of the human imagination, Lewis deplored the increasing gulf between the ordinary reader and the subtleties of criticism. Although he strongly advocated the teaching of English literature in schools, he feared that examinations and degree systems would widen the gulf because they imply that literary appreciation is a severe discipline accessible only to academics. For such an elite ". . . a good critic will be, as the theologians say, essentially a 'twice-born' critic, one who is regenerate and washed from his Original Taste. They will have no conception, because they have no experience, of spontaneous delight in literature. They will be angry with a true lover of literature who does not take pains to unravel the latest poetic puzzle, and call him a dilettante. Having obtained the freedom of Parnassus at a great price, they will be unable to endure the nonchalance of those who were freeborn."[35] What Lewis meant by spontaneous delight was not popular taste as conditioned and exploited by the various media of mass communication. Rather, he was thinking of readers whose taste is untrained by academics but by no means unconditioned, people who have had access to books and some encouragement to correlate the ideas of beauty and pleasure.

This attitude, explicit or implicit throughout Lewis's criticism, antagonized some of those academics who had struggled and saved money and won scholarships to move from homes without books to the libraries of Oxford and Cambridge. They interpreted Lewis's freeborn nonchalance as the complacency of class consciousness. His theory seemed limited to those whose indulgent families had brought them up with books and leisure. That was indeed his own background, but childhood delight in literature is not limited to an elite in societies with free schools and libraries. In America, Lewis's own Narnian stories are in demand at branch libraries in inner-city neighborhoods as well as in affluent suburbs.

In the estrangement of the literary intelligentsia from the "true lover of literature" Lewis recognized three distinct threats to sound criticism: (1) idolatry, (2) exploitation, and (3) biography. Many scholars venerate criticism, or literature, or something less precise, such as "culture," as an end in itself. The widespread tendency thus to make a religion out of art, or culture, is possibly due to a decline in the vital power of real religion in our society. Criticism taken too seriously as a discipline demands for itself the attention that should be focused on literature. Another danger is that criticism may be exploited to some nonliterary end. Lewis referred not to deliberate propaganda, but to overemphasis on a writer's ideas, as if literature were primarily a vehicle for sociology, politics, or religion. An even more insidious false emphasis, according to Lewis, is in the psychoanalytical criticism that regards the work of art as an ink-blot test, used to explain the author's unconscious. The identification of Freudian symbolism may have nothing to do with literary merit: "For we must remember that a story about a golden dragon plucking the apple of immortality in a garden at the world's end, and a dream about one's pen going through the paper while one scribbles a note, are, in Freudian terms, the same story. But they are not the same as literature."[36] A corollary to the misconception that art may be used to psychoanalyze the author is the premise that biographical information is necessary to explain the work of art. This assumption, which Lewis called "the personal heresy," was the topic of one of his best-known scholarly debates, in which he charged that study of Milton's character is largely irrelevant to the understanding and appreciation of his poetry. He contended that "the personal heresy" is based not so much on psychological theory about composition as on two other factors: first, that more people are interested in gossip than are interested in beauty; and second, that materialists consider any abstraction to be merely subjective fancy, without objective validity. Either of these attitudes depreciates the positive value of the literature itself and therefore undermines the valid judgment of it.[37] Biography, like philosophy or theology or any other department of knowledge, can enrich but must not usurp the genuine function of criticism.

The most direct statement of Lewis's concept of what criticism *should* be and do is an essay originally read as a paper to a college literary society. Its informal setting explains the apparent naïveté and oversimplification that Lewis used with carefully calculated effect. He proposed that there is just one "genuinely critical question: 'Why, and how, should we read this?'"[38]

The answer to the question "Why?" is implicit in Lewis's emphasis on the reader's imaginative response as the touchstone of literature: we should read a work because it gives us pleasure. However, the reader's imagination is probably not as active as the writer's and possibly not as perceptive as the critic's; therefore criticism has the major function of stimulating the reader's latent imaginative powers, "to stir those less conscious elements in him which alone can fully respond to the poem."[39] But the imagination stimulated to respond with pleasure and conditioned by the development of taste may still require instruction in *how* a literary work should be read. Lewis thought that knowledge of the background of a poem— the author's ideas, the general climate of opinion, the differences in language and literary fashion—might not be essential to understanding a work and might not achieve understanding; but such knowledge might serve to enhance understanding or remove causes of misunderstanding. Therefore one of the main emphases throughout his criticism is the importance of seeing each period on its own terms rather than imposing the values of our period on all others.

The genuine critical question is not as simple as it first appears. Understanding *how* to read any particular book depends on identifiable variables, but appreciating *why* it is worth reading depends on the instinctive and the metaphysical levels of human experience, which are united in myth. The concept of mythopoeia explains, in terms of basic human instinct, the relationship of both writer and reader to the work of art. Lewis's application of this concept in his criticism and in his imaginative writing has produced some challenging results. For him myth was the master key to life as well as to literature; with it, he opened many different doors.

Chapter III

THE POWER OF LANGUAGE

> . . . *we should become aware of what we*
> *are doing when we speak, of the ancient,*
> *fragile, and (well used) immensely*
> *potent instruments that words are.* —
> STUDIES IN WORDS

Lewis's concept of myth, which was fundamental to everything he wrote, is a significant factor in his increasing popularity. A generation disillusioned with technology and progress is returning to the roots of our culture, to natural foods, folk arts, and fantasy. Whether Lewis and Tolkien have stimulated the renewed interest in myth or merely contributed to it is debatable. Lewis's own interest, which began with a boyhood love of Norse mythology, was given a new direction by the thinking of a university friend, Owen Barfield. Any facet of myth, in the sense of story, or of *Idea,* involves assumptions about the origins of human thought and language that Lewis attributed to the influence of Barfield.

Barfield and Lewis, both of whom were awarded Oxford scholarships in December 1916, became friends when Lewis returned to the university in January 1919 after war service. In *Surprised By Joy,* Lewis described Barfield as the type of friend who

> . . . disagrees with you about everything. He is not so
> much the *alter-ego* as the anti-self. Of course he shares

your interests; otherwise he would not become your friend at all. But he has approached them all at a different angle. He has read all the right books but has got the wrong thing out of every one. It is as if he spoke your langauge but mispronounced it. How can he be so nearly right and yet, invariably, just not right? . . . Actually (though it never seems so at the time) you modify one another's thought; out of this perpetual dogfight a community of mind and a deep affection emerge. But I think he changed me a good deal more than I him. Much of the thought which he afterward put into *Poetic Diction* had already become mine before that important little book appeared.[1]

The stimulating conflict is illustrated by the first reference to Barfield in the published extracts from Lewis's journal:

. . . we walked to Wadham gardens and sat under the trees. We began with "Christian dreams"; I condemned them—the love dream made a man incapable of real love, the hero dream made him a coward. He took the opposite view, and a stubborn argument followed.[2]

Their compatibility was expressed in Barfield's dedication of *Poetic Diction* to Clive Hamilton (Lewis's pseudonym for his early poetry) with the epigraph "Opposition is true friendship," from Blake's *Marriage of Heaven and Hell*. The records of this friendship in seventeen published letters from Lewis to Barfield show that the relationship continued to be close, mutually stimulating, controversial, often teasing. In one, Lewis referred to the six heavily satirized villains of *That Hideous Strength*: "Did I ever mention that Weston, Devine, Frost, Wither, Curry, and Miss Hardcastle were all portraits of you? (If I didn't, that may have been because it isn't true. By gum, though, wait until I write another story.)"[3] In fact his next story, *The Lion, the Witch and the Wardrobe*, was dedicated by her godfather to Barfield's daughter Lucy, whose name was used for its major character. The figure of the Professor, far from being a satire of Barfield, could be identified as Lewis himself expressing his friend's influence. He assures the two older children that little Lucy's tale about being in Narnia for hours, when she had been away from them less than a minute, is ". . . likely to be true. . . . If there really is a door in this house that leads to some other world . . . I should not be at all surprised to find that that other world had a separate time of its own."[4]

Lewis affirmed the importance of Barfield's ideas in the dedication of his first major critical study, *The Allegory of Love*: "To Owen Barfield, wisest and best of my unofficial teachers." More specifically, in the preface he said: ". . . the friend to whom I have dedicated the book has taught me not to patronize the past, and has trained me to see the present as itself a 'period.' I desire for myself no higher function than to be one of the instruments whereby his theory and practice in such matters may become more widely effective."[5] This attitude toward the past and the present is based on a theory of the development of language that Barfield delineated in two books written during the early years of his friendship with Lewis, *History in English Words* and *Poetic Diction.*[6] According to Barfield, poetic diction is closest to the original concrete meaning of language. He argued that development has been from the figurative toward the abstract. For example, the theory that *pneuma* or *spiritus,* originally meaning "breath" or "wind," was employed as a metaphor to mean "the principle of life within man or animal" assumes an advanced degree of abstraction; it is more logical to assume that "breath," "wind," and "principle of life" are later distinctions and subtleties discovered by the intellect in the original single concept of *spiritus*.[7] The original concrete figurative language seems metaphorical now because the process of abstraction has obliterated the original unity of meaning, which Barfield considered inherent rather than invented:

> It is these "footsteps of nature" whose noise we hear alike in primitive language and in the finest metaphors of poets. Men do not *invent* these mysterious relations between separate external objects, and between objects and feelings or ideas, which it is the function of poetry to reveal. . . . The language of primitive men reports them as direct perceptual experience. The speaker has observed a unity, and is not therefore himself conscious of *relation*. But we, in the development of consciousness, have lost the power to see this one as one. . . . it is the language of poets, in so far as they create true metaphors, which must *restore* this unity conceptually, after it has been lost from perception.[8]

This is the basis of the development of poetic diction: language that achieves as much as possible of unified and concrete meaning. As meaning becomes fossilized in the evolution of human thought, the poetic imagination must revive the language by deliberately creating through metaphor the unity that the primitive imagination perceived.

The metaphoric basis of language is a dominant theme in Lewis's first space-fiction novel, *Out of the Silent Planet*. The idea that our planet—controlled by evil—is silent, unable to communicate, is emphasized by the role of a philologist, Ransom, as spokesman, advocate, or intercessor for the human race. The Malacandrian way of life is revealed through Ransom's gradual comprehension of their language. He learns that each of the three species has its own language but all study that of the *hrossa* because, being the most poetic, it expresses ideas most powerfully. Since neither Weston, the scientist, nor Devine, the entrepreneur, has learned more than a pidgin variety of Malacandrian, Ransom must interpret when Weston makes his speech of self-justification before the highest authority, Oyarsa. Ransom has difficulty in translating Weston's abstractions into the concrete Malacandrian terms. The scientist not only speaks a parody of technical jargon, but also is out of touch with the physical realities of the creation he claims to understand. For Weston's introductory "'To you I may seem a vulgar robber, but I bear on my shoulders the destiny of the human race,'" Ransom finds his own version rather unsatisfactory: "'Among us, Oyarsa, there is a kind of *hnau* who will take other *hnaus'* food and—things, when they are not looking. He says he is not an ordinary one of that kind. He says what he does now will make very different things happen to those of our people who are not yet born.'"[9] This contrast is reminiscent of Gulliver's attempts to explain European customs in other languages. Just as the Houyhnhnms have no word for "lie" and can express the concept only with "to say the thing that is not," so the Malacandrians, having no abstraction meaning "evil," use the figurative word "bent" as the opposite of "good." But the difference between these examples is as important as the similarity: Swift was merely calling attention to the contrast between Houyhnhnm and human values, while Lewis was also making a point about language itself. The literal meaning of "bent" makes its metaphorical sense much more precise and powerful than the vague term "evil."

The importance of language per se is further developed in the story of Ransom's second extraterrestrial journey. He speculates that he is being sent to Perelandra because he already knows the language, which he calls Old Solar, "originally a common speech for all rational creatures inhabiting the planets of our system, . . . lost on our own world, when our whole tragedy took place."[10] The philologist hero is much more than a convenience. In contrast to the materialist aim of Weston, Ransom's professional pursuit is the fundamental meaning of language. Although he and the green lady of Perelandra can communicate in speech, they are often bewildered as they use words in different ways. Their attempts to understand each other dramatize the tension between abstract and concrete, between metaphor and reality. When Ransom speaks of a long time, the lady learns a new concept: "'You think times have lengths. A night is always a night whatever you do in it, as from this tree to that is always so many paces whether you take them quickly or slowly. I suppose that is true in a way. But the waves do not always come at equal distances.'"[11] She realizes that the relationship between time and length in one world may not apply equally in another. Ransom himself comes to this realization while struggling against the conviction that he must fight Weston's body in order to prevent evil from corrupting the first mother of Perelandra. When the Voice reminds him that his name is "Ransom," the surname derived from "Ranolf's son" becomes more than a pun or play on words: "All in a moment of time he perceived that what was, to human philologists, a merely accidental resemblance of two sounds, was in truth no accident. The whole distinction between things accidental and things designed, like the distinction between fact and myth, was purely terrestrial."[12] In this context, the philologist represents the first Adam's naming the creatures as well as the second Adam's redeeming man. The power of language is no more accidental than the creation itself.

The same theme is prominent in the third and last Ransom novel, *That Hideous Strength*. The title comes from a description by Sir David Lindsay (one of the Scottish medieval poets praised by Lewis) of the Tower of Babel:

> The Shadow of that hyddeous strength
> Sax myle and more it is of length.

This epigraph stresses the identification of human corruption with corruption of language. The novel (set on our own planet, in an English university town) concerns the conflict between a small Christian community under the leadership of Ransom and a politically powerful institute of applied science dedicated to the control and manipulation of society. Both sides want to make contact with Merlin, whose anticipated return brings about the crisis of the plot. Ransom has the advantage as a Latin and Celtic scholar also familiar with Old Solar, which he expects Merlin to understand or at least recognize as a language of power. He has taught Dr. Dimble, the middle-aged professor of English, to speak in the Great Tongue:

> And Dimble . . . raised his head, and great syllables of words that sounded like castles came out of his mouth. . . . The voice did not sound like Dimble's own: it was as if the words spoke themselves through him from some strong place at a distance—or as if they were not words at all but present operations of God, the planets, and the Pendragon. For this was the language spoken before the Fall and beyond the Moon, and the meanings were not given to the syllables by chance, or skill, or long tradition, but truly inherent in them as the shape of the great Sun is inherent in the little waterdrop. This was Language herself, as she first sprang at Maledil's bid-

ding out of the molten quicksilver of the star called Mercury on Earth, But Viritrilbia in Deep Heaven.[13]

Such language is the antithesis of that used by the directors of the National Institute for Coordinated Experiments (N.I.C.E.). When a young sociologist asks what job he is being recruited for, the Director replies: "'Everyone in the Institute feels that his own work is not so much a departmental contribution to an end already defined as a moment or grade in the progressive self-definition of an organic whole.'"[14] Since Wither always speaks in this jargon, he is slower than the psychologist Frost to recognize the signs of disaster during an N.I.C.E. banquet:

He had never expected the speech to have any meaning as a whole and for a long time the familiar catchwords rolled on in a manner which did not disturb the expectation of his ear. He thought that . . . even a very small false step would deprive both the speaker and the audience of even the power to pretend that he was saying anything in particular. But as long as that border was not crossed, he rather admired the speech. . . . He looked down the room again. They were attending too much, always a bad sign. Then came the sentence, "The surrogates exemplanted in a continual of porous variations."[15]

This speech is the beginning of Merlin's defeat of the N.I.C.E. The organization has made the fatal mistake of disregarding the importance of language in communicating with him:

"This throws a quite unexpected burden on our resources," said Wither to Frost. . . . "I must confess I had not anticipated any serious difficulty about language."

"We must get a Celtic scholar," said Frost. "We are regrettably weak on the philological side."[16]

Their need to advertise for a Celtic scholar to speak to the tramp whom they have mistaken for Merlin gives the real Merlin easy access to their headquarters. In effect the turning point of the plot hinges on the power of language.

In Lewis's final novel, *Till We Have Faces,* the importance of language is stressed not in the plot but in the complex mode of its first-person narration. Queen Orual of Glome explains that her story is written in Greek, which she learned from her slave tutor, since she hopes that it may be found by a traveler and taken to Greece, where there is freedom of speech even about the gods. But she points out also that all names of people and places are in the language of Glome. This opposition, first intimated in terms of language, between the culture of Greece and that of Glome is one of the many thematic contrasts throughout the novel. The fact that Orual and her youngest sister, Istra, call each other by Greek names—Maia and Psyche—is a linguistic equivalent of the dominant duality: the distinction between appearance and reality. (The identification of *Maia* with the Buddhist *Maya,* which is corroborated by her use of the veil, emphasizes this theme.[17]) Orual's purpose in writing her story is to make this distinction as she charges the gods with deceiving men. At the end she realizes the difficulty of her undertaking:

> Lightly men talk of saying what they mean. Often when he was teaching me to write in Greek the Fox would say, "Child, to say the very thing you really mean, the whole of it, nothing more or less or other than what you really mean; that's the whole art and joy of words." A glib

saying. When the time comes to you at which you will be forced at last to utter the speech which has lain at the centre of your soul for years, which you have, all that time, idiot-like, been saying over and over, you'll not talk about joy of words. I saw well why the gods do not speak to us openly, nor let us answer. Till that word can be dug out of us, why should they hear the babble that we think we mean? How can they meet us face to face till we have faces?[18]

The right words, according to Lewis, are more likely to be those of the poet than those of the philosopher, because poetic language is closest to original meaning.

Lewis demonstrated "the art and joy of words" throughout his children's series. On the most obvious level, although English children can understand and speak the language of Narnia, it is not taken for granted that Narnian animals can do so. They receive this power at the creation, lose it when enchanted by the White Witch, and regain it after the sacrifice of Aslan. The enslaved animals of Calormen cannot speak, and the bad giants speak meaningless words of twenty syllables each, a detail reminiscent of Dante's Nimrod as well as the N.I.C.E. Another example of the negation of language's purpose and power is the speech of the Duffers, whose trite and meaningless catchwords and phrases parody the jargon of mass communication:

> "That's right, that's right," said the Chief Voice. "You don't see us. And why not? Because we're invisible."
> "Keep it up, Chief, keep it up," said the Other Voices. "You're talking like a book. They couldn't ask for a better answer than that."[19]

For Lewis such linguistic parodies indicated not just a failure to communicate any real meaning but a fundamental flaw at the depths of the imagination.

Another way in which the mythic significance of language is stressed is in the connotative names of the characters. This familiar convention is given a deeper dimension by Aslan's reaction when Mr. Beaver objects to the White Witch's calling herself Queen of Narnia. "'Peace, Beaver,' said Aslan. 'All names will soon be restored to their proper owners.'"[20] The four children have names that suit them: Peter the leader, Edmund the follower, Susan the practical sister, and Lucy the imaginative one. The two who must be converted, Eustace Scrubb and Jill Pole, call each other by their drab surnames. The good kings of Narnia have euphonious names like Caspian, Rilian, and Tirian, while the worst is Miraz, whose chief advisers are Glozelle and Sopespian. The good Dwarfs have rough, sturdy names like Trumpkin and Trufflehunter, while the enemy Calormenes are Arsheesh and Lasaraleen. Some of the animals' names are onomatopoetic, like Reepicheep the mouse and Hwin the mare; and some names are descriptive, like Queen Prunaprismia or Puddleglum, the pessimistic Marshwiggle. In general, the names of both people and places are as original and evocative as Cair Paravel (the castle of the Narnian kings).

The power of language is suggested also by the use of refrains. In *The Lion, the Witch and the Wardrobe,* Mr. Beaver first whispers a secret: "'They say Aslan is on the move—perhaps has already landed.'"[21] Repetition of "Aslan is on the move" thrills the reader as it does the children even before they know who Aslan is. In *The Horse and His Boy,* the escape from Calormen is encouraged by the repeated signal, "Narnia and the North." Even more haunting is the call of the friends of Aslan, "Further up and further in." At the end of *The Last Battle* this rallying cry marks stages in the crescendo of action and imagery. Such refrains function almost as spells; but when Lucy reads the Magician's book containing real spells, the author says: "Nothing will induce me to tell you what they were."[22] Some language is too powerful.

This emphasis on the power of language, traceable as a leitmotif throughout Lewis's imaginative writing, operates also in his critical and scholarly works. One of his most consistent aims was to distinguish between the meanings that words have accrued over the centuries and to strip them back to the native grain of their meaning for the original audience. In *The Allegory of Love*, Lewis's primary purpose of "reconstructing that long-lost state of mind for which the allegorical love poem was a natural mode of expression"[23] required careful attention to the metaphoric power of words. He noted, for instance, the "coming and going between the natural and the allegorical senses of his 'love' that makes Usk [a fifteenth-century poet] so profoundly interesting to the historian of sentiment."[24] In Latin literature, Lewis found the names of picturable deities such as Venus used instead of abstractions like "love," in passages ranging from lyric poetry to the prose of Caesar. He concluded that

> . . . a distinction which is fundamental for us—the distinction, namely, between an abstract universal and a living spirit—was only vaguely and intermittently present to the Roman mind. Nor need we despair of recovering, for a moment, this point of view, if we remember the strange border-line position which a notion such as "Nature" occupies to-day in the mind of an imaginative and unphilosophical person who has read many books of popularized science. It is something more than a personification and less than a myth, and ready to be either or both as the stress of argument demands.[25]

These two words—"love" and "Nature"—are important examples of changes from concrete meaning to widely differentiated abstraction. Lewis analyzes both of them in two books published in 1960, twenty-five years after *The Allegory of Love.*

In *The Four Loves,* the main focus is on the psychological, moral, and spiritual implications of different types of love: Affection, Friendship, Eros, and Charity, each related in complex degrees to what Lewis called "Gift-love" and "Need-love." But throughout the book, he called attention to the metaphoric power of the words. "Affection" in Greek was *storge,* especially the relationship of parents to offspring. Lewis identified parental love as "the original form of the thing as well as the central meaning of the word. The image we must start with is that of a mother nursing a baby, a bitch or a cat with a basketful of puppies or kittens."[26] In another context he explained a key word by ending rather than starting with an image. In making the transition from the natural loves to love for God, Lewis affirmed: "It remains certainly true that all natural loves can be inordinate. *Inordinate* does not mean 'insufficiently cautious.' Nor does it mean 'too big.' It is not a quantitative term. It is probably impossible to love any human being simply 'too much'. . . the question whether we are loving God or the earthly Beloved 'more' is not, so far as concerns our Christian duty, a question about the comparative intensity of two feelings. The real question is, which (when the alternative comes) do you serve, or choose, or put first?"[27] *Inordinate* is thus shown to mean "out of order," a precise figurative concept rather than an abstraction.

In *Studies In Words,* a book based on Cambridge lectures about changes in meaning that make the understanding of older literature difficult, Lewis began with "Nature," as related to the Greek *phusis,* Latin *natura,* and English *kind.* He traced fifteen different senses of the word, beginning with "sort," "type," or "essential characteristic": "nature shares a common base with *nasci* (to be born); with the noun *natus* (birth); with *natio* (not only a race or nation but the name of the birth-goddess). . . . there is obviously some idea of a thing's *natura* as its original or 'innate' character."[28] With increasing abstraction, meanings proliferate. For instance, the "innate character" of something may be contrasted with man's manipulation of it. In this sense,

> a yew-tree is *natural* before the topiarist has carved it. . . . This distinction between the uninterfered with and the interfered with will not probably recommend itself to the philosopher. It may be held to enshrine a very primitive, an almost magical or animistic, conception of causality. . . . What keeps the contrast alive, however, is the daily experience of men as practical, not speculative, beings. The antithesis between unreclaimed land and the cleared, drained, fenced, ploughed, sown, and weeded field—between the unbroken and the broken horse—between the fish as caught and the fish opened, cleaned, and fried—is forced upon us every day. . . . If ants had a language they would, no doubt, call their anthill an artifact and describe the brick wall in its neighbourhood as a *natural* object. *Nature* in fact would be for them all that was not "ant-made."[29]

Philosophers might also object to the sense of "Nature" identified particularly with eighteenth- and nineteenth-century poetry, but Lewis justified this common use on the grounds that its contrast with the man-made urban environment is something most people genuinely feel. "People know pretty well what they mean by it and sometimes use it to communicate what would not easily be communicable in other ways."[30] But the abstraction can be ridiculous if it is used with no sensitivity to its original meaning, as in Lewis's example of "a railway poster which advertised Kent as 'Nature's home.'"[31]

All the words Lewis traced in this study are related in some way to man's perceptions of his own "nature," collectively or individually: *sad, wit, free, sense, simple, conscious, conscience*. The histories of such words are most likely to illustrate subtle and complex changes from original simple meaning, in which the material and immaterial senses were indistinguishable, to increasingly self-conscious abstractions. Lewis's main purpose was to call modern students' attention to the changes, to show them *how* to read literature of different periods. He included a chapter, "At the Fringe of Language," to elucidate a principle about the use of words: he pointed out that the vocabulary of praise, abuse, and expression of emotion in general is being diminished by the fading of metaphoric meaning. Words formerly "stimulated emotion because they also stimulated something else: imagination."[32] "Sickening," "villain," and "bitch" no longer evoke images.[33] Many modern writers, according to Lewis, lack his beloved Spenser's "profound sympathy with . . . the fundamental tendencies of the human imagination as such."[34]

Because language is based on the most fundamental processes of the human consciousness, the history of the language has important implications for history as a whole. It was this aspect of Owen Barfield's theory that Lewis wanted to promote. Their mutual friend Tolkien expressed this conviction when he related the origin of fairy tales to the origin of language in the perception of concrete meaning. The key to the significance of the fairy story is in the double meaning of *spell* as story and as incantation.[35] It is interesting to note that the word *gospel*, the "good spell," incorporates both these meanings; by implication, the present-day translation "good news" reflects a change in the human imagination. (The complete *Oxford English Dictionary* gives a fascinating analysis of the history of *gospel*.) We have retained the meaning of *story* only, since we are now more readily persuaded by news than by spells. However, the word *spell* reveals, in what Barfield might call a fossilized form, the fundamental power of language: the idea that to pronounce the right name is to exercise power—to say the letters in the right order is to cast a spell.

Barfield's theory of the history of language as a movement from concrete metaphor to abstraction illustrates that history is not necessarily evolutionary in the sense of continual improvement. He considered the "progressive" view of history responsible for misunderstanding the past: this assumption has resulted in too much emphasis on those features of the past that have survived and too little emphasis on features perhaps more important that have been lost. Lewis, following Barfield, attempted to understand past literature on its own terms rather than to repudiate what seemed "dated" and to praise the "up-to-date." It can be equally difficult, in other ways, to see the literature of one's own period in the right perspective. Lewis noted, for instance, that the contemporary student's inability to scan poetry, which he had observed as a teacher, was parallel to the contemporary poet's use of free verse; but he speculated that there might be no direct relationship: "More probably the ignorance, and the deliberate abandonment, of accentual meters are correlative phenomena, and both the result of some revolution in our whole sense of rhythm—a revolution of great importance reaching deep down into the unconscious and even perhaps into the blood."[36] He made no attempt to identify this revolution more precisely; it serves as an illustration of our ignorance of the pattern of history. Lewis believed that there *is* a pattern, which can be apprehended imaginatively through myth—Arthurian, Malacandrian, Narnian, or some other. Art can imply but logic cannot prove what stage of the pattern has been reached in actual history. He considered the least dangerous philosophy of history to be "simple Providentialism": "It is a method which saves minor historians from writing a great deal of nonsense and compels them to get on with the story."[37]

In his fascination with the mythic power of language, in his stimulating analyses of changes in meaning from the metaphoric to the abstract, Lewis was continually propagating Barfield's theories, as he had intended to do. By showing that the history of language involves losses as well as gains, he suggested that the same is true for the history of our literature and our culture as a whole. The only way to understand any of these patterns is to realize that they are, fundamentally, mythic. In a letter to Barfield in 1939, Lewis predicted the increased interest in this approach during the succeeding forty years:

> You could hardly expect the man in the T.L.S. to know the esoteric doctrine of myths.
>
> By the bye, we now need a new word for the "science of the nature of myths," since "mythology" has been appropriated for the myths themselves. Would "mythonomy" do? I am quite serious. If your views are not a complete error, this subject will become more important; and it's worth while trying to get a good word before they invent a beastly one. "Mytho-logic" (noun) wouldn't be bad, but people would read it as an adjective. I have also thought of "mythopoetics" (cf. "metaphysics"), but that leads to "a mythopoecian," which is frightful; whereas "a mythonomer" (better still "The Mythonomer Royal") is nice. Or shall we just invent a new word—like "gas." (Nay sir, I meant nothing.)[38]

The blend of gravity and humor in the letter is typical. He took the subject seriously, but he never took himself

46

too seriously. Had the post of Mythonomer Royal been established, he would have recommended Tolkien or Barfield for it rather than himself. Lewis was right about the increasing importance of the subject. Now Barfield, as a trustee of Lewis's estate, continues the interdependent relationship that began more than half a century ago. Barfield was a catalyst for a chain reaction in Lewis's approach to literature.

Chapter IV

THE REAL RENAISSANCE

> *. . . while men often throw away*
> *irreplaceable wealth, they not*
> *infrequently escape what seemed*
> *inevitable dangers, not knowing that*
> *they have done either nor how they did*
> *it.*—ENGLISH LITERATURE IN THE
> SIXTEENTH CENTURY

C. S. Lewis played more roles than most of his readers realize: poet, literary historian, critic, essayist, religious apologist, novelist, and teller of fairy tales. All his writing reveals his fundamental convictions about the significance of myth and the power of language, but these ideas are most clearly formulated in the literary history and criticism of his professional writing, which is familiar to few readers other than English-majors. Many Lewis admirers know so little of the literature he writes about that they never venture into the territory where he was most at home, thus missing an important aspect of his thought and lacking perspective for his other work.

The significance of Lewis's scholarly criticism was first recognized by a scholarly and perceptive reviewer of his first major book, *The Allegory of Love*: "No one could read it without seeing all literature a little differently for ever after."[1] This judgment acknowledges one of Lewis's chief aims: placing works of literature in their historical context. In his major scholarly studies, he concentrated on explaining to modern readers what the words themselves, the images, the forms, and the themes meant to the writers and their original audiences. In *The Allegory of Love,* Lewis analyzed the medieval idea of courtly love, the origins of allegory as a literary form, the mutations of the form in medieval love poems, and the transmutation of both form and sentiment in Spenser's *The Faerie Queene.* In *English Literature in the Sixteenth Century* he identified the medieval background of the century, the influences of the humanist movement, and the transformation in style and content in the last quarter of the century. In *A Preface to Paradise Lost* he attempted "to hinder hindrances" to the modern reader's appreciation by explaining the distinctive features of the epic form, the characteristics of Milton's style, and the "hierarchical conception of the universe" on which the poem is based.[2] In *The Discarded Image,* he provided for students of medieval and Renaissance literature a detailed analysis of the intellectual Model of the Universe that provided the imagery and the themes of European literature until the nineteenth century. In *Studies in Words,* he narrowed the focus to the strictly "lexical and historical," tracing the changes in eight key words whose meanings are central to the literature of various periods. Such studies may sound interesting only to the English-majors for whom Lewis originally developed them as university lectures, but their implications are wider than the curriculum or the discipline.

Lewis always looked at literature not only within its original historical context but also from the perspective of the timeless. He argued repeatedly that the critic or reader who judges a book solely by the criteria of his own era does not understand either the author's intentions or his own perceptions: failing to recognize the distinctive features of other periods, he also fails to perceive his own period as limited and transient. Such a reader is guilty of the "chronological snobbery" that Lewis was taught by Owen Barfield to condemn: the attitude that what is best in earlier literature is what is most "modern." For what is now "modern" taste will change, as language is constantly changing; contemporary attitudes are not absolutes. Lewis often pointed out that our "modern" assumptions may lead us to ask the wrong questions. Instead of wondering how audiences for centuries could have enjoyed epic and allegory and fantasy, perhaps we should consider why so many of us do not. The important task of the critic is to distinguish for us between the particular and the universal in any work of art. Lewis introduced *The Allegory of Love,* subtitled "A Study in Medieval Tradition," with a defense of his purpose that would apply to almost all of his literary studies: "Neither the form nor the sentiment of this old poetry has passed away without leaving indelible traces on our minds. We shall understand our present, and perhaps even our future, the better if we can succeed, by an effort of the historical imagination, in reconstructing that long-lost state of mind for which the allegorical love poem was a natural mode of expression."[3] Lewis's constant focus on features of the past in relationship to the present and (perhaps) the future is what makes his readers "see all literature a little differently for ever after."

The emphasis implicit or explicit in all Lewis's criticism is that mythopoeia is the essence of literature. His distinctions between the particular styles, forms, and ideas of one period and the universal appeal of all great literature are in terms of the imagination's response to myth. The result is that many academic or popular generalizations about periods and authors are reversed, remodeled, or transcended.

The Allegory of Love was Lewis's first and remains his greatest achievement in critical scholarship. In attempting to revitalize medieval literature for the modern reader, he set forth all the premises of his future work. One of these was his conviction that our stereotypes of the "gothic" were mistakes inherited from the Renaissance humanists. Recent historians have developed such new stereotypes as the twelfth-century Renaissance to replace the old ones, but Lewis repudiated the idea of "rebirth." He argued that the Middle Ages, having more cultural coherence than our own age, had also more genuine vitality in the arts because these were derived directly from what was considered most significant in human life.

Allegorical love poetry depended on the tradition of courtly love. Lewis compared this essential relationship between art and life to the relationship in the nineteenth century between the form of the novel and the tradition of romantic courtship and marriage: novelists as varied as Austen and Scott, Eliot and the Brontës, Dickens and Thackeray, Meredith and Trollope, James and Galsworthy, all accepted a code which their readers understood and shared. The implication is that the diffusion of the novel form in the twentieth century reflects corresponding fragmentation of our societal patterns. The Middle Ages could create a literary form from the period's coherent civilization. Pattern or form is what distinguishes creation from chaos, human imagination from animal instinct, civilization from barbarism; therefore, the most highly developed pattern characterizes and testifies to the highest degree of civilization. In this argument, Lewis stressed that the medieval tradition of courtly love was an intricate and subtle pattern superimposed on (though not contradictory to) instinct. It was a sentiment and attitude completely unknown in the classical and so-called "dark" ages (pp. 3–12), derived in complex ways from the feudal code and the teaching of the medieval church (pp. 12–22). The vitality of Chaucer's *Troilus and*

Criseyde, for instance, derived from the extreme subtlety, sophistication, and delicacy of Chaucer's scholastic and aristocratic world (p. 77), a pattern of life which gave form to a work of art. Lewis disagreed with the critics who have praised *Troilus,* like the *Canterbury Tales,* for "modernity," acclaiming Chaucer as a forerunner of the novelists. He insisted that the medievalism of the poem afforded the unity that results in imaginative appeal and universality. The *ideal* of courtly love gives the love story significance on two levels: it is theoretically consistent as well as psychologically sound. The story is more powerful as story because of its place in the medieval system (pp. 176–97).

Unity in the relationship between patterns of life and art is one of the emphases in Lewis's reversal of stereotypes about the Middle Ages; another is the importance of stylistic unity. Most moderns think of medieval literature, in contrast to classical, as lacking any unity of style and focus. The elaborate rhetorical ornamentation and frequent digressions on theology, astrology, medicine, metaphysics, or courtly love irritate the reader who wants to get on with the story, as Lewis always urged him to do. Lewis justified these features in terms of the heightened impact of unity in diversity, which stimulates and satisfies a basic need of the imagination:

> Unity of interest is not "classical"; it is not foreign to any art that has ever existed or ever can exist in the world. Unity in diversity if possible—failing that, mere unity, as a second best—these are the norms for all human work, given, not by the ancients, but by the nature of consciousness itself. . . . If medieval works often lack unity, they lack it not because they are medieval, but because they are, so far, bad. . . . medieval art . . . failed of unity because it attempted vast designs with inadequate re-

sources. When the design was modest—as in *Gawaine and the Green Knight* or in some Norman parish churches—or when the resources were adequate—as in Salisbury Cathedral and the *Divine Comedy*—then medieval art attains a unity of the highest order, because it embraces the greatest diversity of subordinated detail. (pp. 141–42)

For Lewis, what was most medieval was most universal, in style as well as in form.

The climax of Lewis's reassessment of medieval literature is his treatment of *The Faerie Queene.* If MacDonald's *Phantastes* "baptized" Lewis's imagination, it was Spenser's allegorical epic fantasy that "confirmed" him in the doctrine of mythopoeia. Its form is not allegory but Italian romantic epic adapted for allegorical purposes. For the fullest understanding of Spenser, one should have the wide experience of Italian epic that Lewis tried to distil in a few tantalizing pages (pp. 298–303). It is necessary to recognize the type in order to appreciate Spenser's variations; they have a common structure and surface in their series of fantastic adventures, but beneath the surface their levels of meaning are divergent. The Italian epic based its fantasy on realistic details of everyday life, with a deeper background of heroic legend (pp. 308–9). Spenser, on the other hand, used the romantic epic allegorically on several different levels. The level first apparent is not so much allegory as symbol: the knight, the lady, the dragon's mouth, the ghosts, the hungry wolves are not imaginary expressions of facts in the natural world but realities that express the supernatural world. "What lies next beneath the surface in Spenser's poem is the world of popular imagination: almost, a popular mythology. . . . Spenser's real concern [is] the primitive or instinctive mind, with all its terrors and ecstasies" (p. 312). This level of meaning has more enduring significance than the allegories of knights combatting Sin and Error or of the Virgin Queen restoring the glories of Arthur's reign. *The Faerie Queene*, virtually unknown to modern readers, was for Lewis the touchstone for imaginative literature.

The treatment of Spenser as the culmination of medieval literary tradition served not only to vindicate the Middle Ages but also to repudiate the Renaissance. In the conclusion of *The Allegory of Love*, Lewis defined Spenser's position as the "great mediator between the Middle Ages and the modern poets, the man who saved us from the catastrophe of too thorough a renaissance" (p. 360). Nearly twenty years later this concept was the basis of his contribution to the Oxford history series, *English Literature in the Sixteenth Century, Excluding Drama.* In a brief analysis on the dust jacket, the publishers said: "The pattern which emerges is, in some ways, unexpected." It is difficult to understand how anyone familiar with Lewis's work could find the pattern in any way unexpected.

In one of his earliest articles Lewis had commented that the scholar and critic W. P. Ker did not believe "too intemperately in the Renaissance."[4] Although the Renaissance idea had already been attacked, it persisted in literary history and criticism with sufficient tenacity for Lewis to use it as a straw man in his argument. He once startled a friend whom he met on a walk by exclaiming, "I have just proved that the Renaissance never happened!" In contrast to the stereotype of a sharp break between the Middle Ages and the sixteenth century, Lewis found more continuity than discontinuity. The distinctly new features of the period labeled "Renaissance" seemed to him spiritually and imaginatively retrogressive; if these new elements had become dominant, the result would, in his view, have been catastrophic rather than regenerative. For a standard history of English literature, a pattern that makes the Renaissance insignificant is indeed unusual.

As part of a series, *English Literature in the Sixteenth Century* is obviously different in purpose from *The Allegory of Love*. Instead of developing with an unlimited choice of materials a limited theme of his own choosing, Lewis was responsible for a comprehensive analysis of all aspects of the literature of a prescribed century. The publishers announced that "pains have been taken to prevent the concept of 'the Renaissance' from imposing a false unity on this complicated period." In fact, through Lewis's attack on the "Renaissance," a different unity was imposed on, or revealed in, the great diversity of the sixteenth century. The general principle of chronology in a survey must be supplemented by some subordinate principle based on relationships of kind rather than of time; Lewis's arrangement did not avoid but rejected the Renaissance stereotype, not covertly but overtly, as set forth in the inimitable opening paragraph:

> The rough outline of our literary history in the sixteenth century is not very difficult to grasp. At the beginning we find a literature still medieval in form and spirit. . . . As the century proceeds, new influences arise: changes in our knowledge of antiquity, new poetry from Italy and France, new theology, new movements in philosophy or science. . . . In England the characteristic disease of late medieval poetry, its metrical disorder, is healed: but replaced, for the most part, by a lifeless and laboured regularity. . . . The mid-century is an earnest, heavy-handed, common-place age: a drab age. Then in the last quarter of the century, the unpredictable happens. . . . Fantasy, conceit, paradox, colour, incantation return. Youth returns. The fine frenzies of ideal love and ideal

war are readmitted. . . . Nothing in the earlier history of
our period would have enabled the sharpest observer to
foresee this transformation.[5]

This summary establishes the major sections of the volume: Book I, Late Medieval; Book II, "Drab"; Book III, "Golden"; and an Epilogue, New Tendencies. The plan follows Lewis's thesis that the genuine spirit of medieval literature was lost in the twilight shades of the so-called *renascentia* and was later rediscovered and transformed by the Elizabethans. With a reversal of conventional literary history, Lewis concluded that the influence of the Elizabethans and the metaphysicals combined to destroy the "medieval liberty" of poetry.

Lewis's emphasis on imaginative freedom as the essence of literature and his identification of this freedom with the medieval spirit form the unifying theme of *English Literature in the Sixteenth Century.* In developing this theme, he described the reign of James IV of Scotland as a period in which "all that is bright, reckless, and fantastical in the late medieval tradition finds superb expression" (p. 66). He discussed the little-known poets Gavin Douglas and William Dunbar, emphasizing their imaginative power and sophisticated artistry respectively, in order to demonstrate that what was typically medieval is also most universal in its appeal. Praising the "cheerful briskness" of Douglas's translation of the *Aeneid*, Lewis judged that our impressions are distorted by the misconceptions of the neoclassicals,

> . . . that fatal "classical" misconception of all ancient poets which the humanists have fastened upon our education—the spectral solemnity, the gradus epithets, the dictionary language, the decorum which avoids every contact with the senses and the soil. To read the Latin

again with Douglas's version fresh in our minds is like
seeing a favourite picture after it has been cleaned. Half
the "richness" and "sobriety" which we have been taught
to admire turns out to have been only dirt; the "brown
trees" disappear and where the sponge has passed the
glowing reds, the purples, and the transparent blues
leap into life. (p. 84)

This suggestion of the beauty of medieval stained glass,
whose secret has been lost, is typical of the impression
Lewis conveyed of Scottish literature at the close of the
Middle Ages.

In turning to English literature of the same period,
Lewis felt that he was passing "from civilization into
barbarism" (p. 120). The decline resulted from unim-
aginative imitation of medieval characteristics. Lewis argued that mere stylistic imitation, whether of medieval or
of classical models, produces a travesty of the original
spirit. The classical studies of the first humanists had
only bad effects on their vernacular poetry: "Their language is undistinguished, their sentences untrussed,
their thought commonplace and indistinct. . . . This is
the real midwinter of our poetry; all smudge, blur, and
scribble, without a firm line or a clear colour anywhere"
(p. 127). He considered the prose of the period even
worse, except that which preserved the chivalric romances, "the ripe fruits of the Middle Ages; . . . their
popularity may have helped to save us from a too complete break with the past" (p. 156).

The image of medieval brightness blurred by the humanists is the perspective from which Lewis viewed the
first major division of the sixteenth century, which he
labeled the "Drab" Age. In the introduction he dis-
claimed any disparagement: "Drab is not used as a dys-
logistic term. It marks a period in which, for good or ill,

poetry has little richness. . . . The good work is neat and temperate, the bad flat and dry" (p. 64). But the disparagement is so obvious that Lewis must have been aware of it. He began his study of the "Drab" Age with a chapter on "Religious Controversy and Translation," offering abundant examples of drabness in the usual sense of the word. Sir Thomas More, humanist and orthodox churchman, is shown to be least interesting when he is most humanist and orthodox; of the majority of his controversial writing, Lewis said: "The earliest criticism ever made on these works is recorded by More himself ('The brethren cannot beare that my writing is so long') and it cannot be seriously questioned" (p. 173). What Lewis found most delightful in More were his affinities with the medievals on the one hand and with the Elizabethan pamphleteers on the other. His humanistic rhetoric is interspersed with "the gusto of . . . hard-hitting, racy, street-corner abuse" (p. 175), with homely, comic passages whose "race and pith and mere Englishry are the great redeeming features of his prose" (p. 180). More made his great contribution to our literature not as a humanist but as a mythmaker, the creator of *Utopia,* which Lewis saw not as a philosophical treatise but as an imaginary world: "a holiday work, a spontaneous overflow of intellectual high spirits, a revel of debate, paradox, comedy and (above all) of invention" (p. 169). The fact that More's creation has contributed a word to the language illustrates Lewis's concept of the power of myth.

Comparing the prose and verse of the period, Lewis concluded that the prose writers often escaped the worst features of "Drab" style because they concentrated on matter rather than manner. In discussing a wide range of writers, he constantly associated Drabness with a kind of humanism that stifled the shaping power of imagination. In trying to counteract the conventional critical bias in favor of humanism, Lewis praised some of the humanists for unconventional reasons. He attributed the reality and charm of Roger Ascham's *The Schoolmaster* to the fact that the tutor of Queen Elizabeth wrote about what he knew and loved best: "Even in his driest or most perverse pages, we feel the presence of a humanity which his humanism could never quite defeat" (p. 282).

After repudiating the concept of *renascentia* as a flowering of English literature, Lewis traced the transition from "Drab" to "Golden" as a revival of medieval matter and manner. In describing Hobbes's translation of Castiglione's *Courtier,* he said:

> . . . we see the air and fire of youth chasing away the staidness of the Drab Age. . . . And he has a right to sound youthful for his book really marks a rejuvenation or re-birth, though a different one from the *renascentia* in its proper sense. He is retrieving, with modifications, the medieval ideal; the knight and lover who might, to our endless loss, have been simply rejected in favour of the half Plutarchan, half Machiavellian, Great Man, is recalled and refashioned and set forward on a new career. . . . And though all is serious, all is graceful, spontaneous, unconstrained. (pp. 305–6)

The most important words here are "spontaneous" and "unconstrained." In contrast to the stereotype of the Renaissance as a release from the shackles of medieval ignorance and dogmatism, Lewis saw in the late sixteenth century a release from the restraints of a slavish classicism.

Lewis found good examples of such classicism in the writing of John Lyly, whose two works of fiction, *Euphues* and *Euphues and His England,* gave to the language of literary criticism the term *euphuism.* The reference is not to the hero but to the author's prose style, characterized by an excess of antithesis, alliteration, balance, rhyme, assonance, and pseudoscientific simile. Lewis considered Lyly's fiction inferior to the medieval mode of storytelling because the author was interested in rhetoric rather than in character or situation, and in fashionable didacticism rather than in genuine moral values (p. 315). But Lyly's plays, unlike his fiction, revived so many of the features of medieval literature that Lewis had to trespass the boundaries of a volume supposed to exclude drama. He saw in Lyly the first glints of gold:

> Lyly as a dramatist is the first writer since the great medievals whose taste we can trust. . . . Having conceived the imaginary world in which most of his plays are set . . . he brings everything into keeping. He is consistently and exquisitely artificial. . . . The lightness of Lyly's touch, the delicacy, the blessed unreality were real advances in civilization. His nymphs and shepherdesses are among the first ladies we have met since the Middle Ages. . . . For in the larger and older sense of the word his genius was essentially poetical and his work "poesie." Here is the "Golden" literature at last. (pp. 316–17)

This passage belies Lewis's reminder at the beginning of the chapter that he did not use the term "Golden" in a eulogistic sense. He insisted that he used it merely to describe poetry that is youthful as opposed to middle-aged, or innocent as opposed to sophisticated, poetry whose appeal is direct rather than indirect. With three concise examples he clarified this distinction: "Marlowe's 'Come live with me' is Golden, Donne's answer to it is not. The rhythm in 'beauty making beautiful old rhyme' is Golden, that in 'Burnt after them to the bottomless pit' is not. Phoebus dancing forth from the oriental gate is a

Golden image; snow coming down to periwig the bald-pate woods is far otherwise" (p. 318).

The practice of the "Golden" poets was based on a theory having so much in common with Lewis's own that it is impossible to take seriously his claim for the objectivity of the term "Golden." Sir Philip Sidney's *Defence of Poesie* must have been the source of the label. Lewis agreed with Sidney's conviction that "the poet, unlike the historian, is not 'captived to the trueth of a foolish world' but can 'deliver a golden'" (p. 320). He stressed that the "Golden" poets derived their inspiration and imaginative freedom from their confidence that the human soul was in contact with the realm of metaphysical truth (pp. 319–21); their stylistic ornamentation was not merely decorative but illustrative of the heightened quality of a "golden" world. In this respect Lewis contrasted the Elizabethans not only with their humanist predecessors but also with his own contemporaries: "Most of the Golden poetry was not primarily intended either to reflect the actual world or to express the personality of the poet. . . . The poets of that age were full of reverence—for God, for kings, for father, for authority—but not of our reverence for the actual" (p. 322). Lewis stressed that the "Golden" writers, particularly Sidney and Spenser, were in fact mythmakers.

Throughout this section of *English Literature in the Sixteenth Century* runs the theme of mythopoeia, the concept of great literature as harmony of form and content, in terms of implicit and universal pattern. For instance, in identifying an Elizabethan prose romance with outstanding imaginative appeal, Lewis said of Lodge's *Margarita*: "Rhetoric . . . is raised to quite a new power. Far from being a mere external decoration, it becomes in the best passages at once an ironic contrast to, and a subtle expression of, the pride and passion of the speakers. If the book is not realistic, it is real; the compulsive imagination of a larger, brighter, bitterer, more dangerous world than ours" (pp. 424–25). This passage could be a Lewis description of a medieval romance, and its last sentence could apply to Tolkien's *The Lord of the Rings.* The emphasis is on the excitement of imaginary worlds, an emphasis also present in Lewis's discussion of one characteristic type of "Golden" poetry, the sonnet sequence. He stressed that the sonnets' relation to the poet's actual experience, to his sincere thoughts, is irrelevant; what matters is the relationship of the poetic elements within each sonnet and among the various sonnets (pp. 489–98). Each sequence creates its own imaginary realm, as supremely illustrated in Shakespeare's sonnets. This point of view conflicts with scholarly aims of arranging the sonnets in chronological order or relating them to Shakespeare's life. Lewis wrote the book before the controversy over opening his patron's grave for new evidence, and he died before the historian A. L. Rowse made his farfetched claim to have identified the "Dark Lady" of the sonnets; he would have disparaged both. He found the unity of the sequence in its variations on the theme of love universal, "the quintessence of all loves whether erotic, parental, filial, amicable, or feudal" (p. 505). These variations on a theme are expressed in meter, language, and rhetorical structure of a formal beauty comparable to the pattern in music: the epitome of "Golden" poetry (pp. 505–8).

In repudiating the generalizations about medieval and Renaissance literature, Lewis had the underlying purpose of reconsidering the major tradition of English literature as a whole. His critical contrast of Sidney and Spenser reveals this purpose clearly: he found in Sidney the distillation of a particular era, whereas he found in Spenser the epitome of the entire English Christian literary and cultural tradition. He discussed Sidney first as representative, Spenser last as transcendent.

Sidney's life and career as the ideal aristocrat, poet, courtier, scholar, and soldier were, for Lewis, relevant to his writing not in terms of biographical data but as indicative of general temper and ethos. In his prose romance, *Arcadia,* Sidney was interested not in the actual world, nor in an ideal world remote from the actual, but in an imaginary world of heightened reality based on the aristocratic concepts of his own society: "In that way the *Arcadia* is a kind of touchstone. What a man thinks of it, far more than what he thinks of Shakespeare or Spenser or Donne, tests the depth of his sympathy with the sixteenth century. For it is a work of distillation. It gathers up what a whole generation wanted to say. The very gallimaufry that it is—medieval, Protestant, pastoral, Stoical, Platonic—made it the more characteristic and, as long as that society lasted, the more satisfactory" (p. 339). Lewis summed up his discussion of Sidney with the idea that the "Golden" poetics was more fundamental than a mere literary fashion: it was the spirit of an age (p. 346).

Spenser, in contrast to Sidney, represented for Lewis not an era but a timeless tradition. Much of his early work was weak because he was following literary fashions, but in *The Faerie Queene* he followed his own instincts and used his great gift of imaginative invention. Lewis introduced this key topic with deceptive simplicity: "He liked looking at the past, the legendary past, and continued to look; and out of it he made not, as we idly say, a dream—for the dreamer takes all he sees to be reality—but a vast, invented structure which other men could walk all round and in and out of for four centuries" (p. 352). Spenser had the power of conceiving inner experiences in terms of the external images and situations of a unified narrative: "For those who can surrender themselves simply to the story Spenser himself will provide guidance enough. The allegory that really matters is unmistakable. . . . They receive the allegory so easily that they forget they have done so. . . . The plan, the story, the invention are triumphant (pp. 388–89). Spenser's creation of the myth of Faerie Land was a supreme example, for Lewis, of myth as the basis of literature.

Lewis's elevation of Spenser to a position second only to Shakespeare and Milton as a major influence in the English tradition could have been no surprise to readers familiar with his earlier criticism. Similarly, the "new tendencies" identified at the end of the sixteenth century had already been pointed out in an earlier essay on John Donne. The last chapter of the history contains an attack on the twentieth-century revival of the metaphysicals at the expense of the Elizabethans. In the early years of this revival, Lewis had been excited by the discovery of Donne, as his friend and fellow student Nevill Coghill recorded in a memoir,[6] but he objected to the popular notions (1) that the metaphysicals were rebels against the artificiality of their predecessors and (2) that they have an immediacy for the modern world that the Elizabethans lack. His definition of metaphysical as "dependent on a calculated breach of decorum"[7] meant that the shock effect resulted from the reader's preference for and expectation of a different kind of imagery. To illustrate the metaphysicals' lack of universality, Lewis cited examples of metaphysical images no longer meaningful, such as the line in Donne's *Second Anniversary* about the released soul who "baits not at the Moone"; he suggested that "to get the effect which Donne intended we should now have to say that she does not stop for petrol or change trains."[8] Such an example of a commonplace modern equivalent was used to discredit the imaginative power of the metaphysicals. Lewis's analysis of the new tendencies was no more objective than his categories of "Drab" and "Golden."

The conclusion of *English Literature in the Sixteenth Century* is that the tradition epitomized in Spenser is now waning:

> Among those who shared, or still share, the culture for which he wrote, and which he helped to create, there is no dispute about his greatness. . . . There may—or may not—come a time when the culture for which Spenser wrote and the culture which is now replacing it can be compared, by men to whom English is a dead language, as coolly as we now compare two periods of ancient Egyptian history. At present it is not possible. We can only say that those who in any degree belong to the old culture still find in the ordered exuberance of the *Faerie Queene* an invigorating refreshment which no other book can supply.[9]

Here Lewis acknowledged that his survey of sixteenth-century literature would be controversial, and he pointed out that such controversy is inevitable as long as English is a living language.

The key to Lewis's concept of the tradition now in decline is the phrase "ordered exuberance." The essence of great literature, according to Lewis, is the synthesis of order and exuberance, of discipline and high spirits. Both aspects of experience involve an imaginative apprehension of the relationship between the actual world and an ideal world; this relationship imposes artistic or ethical order on the exuberance of imagination and, conversely, transforms with imaginative exuberance the order of reality. There is thus a parallel between literature and religion that underlies Lewis's revaluation of "medieval" and "Renaissance," as well as everything else

65

he wrote. It is responsible for the hostility of some of Lewis's detractors and for the devotion of many of his followers. In both camps there are those who misinterpret the paradox of his reverent iconoclasm.

As a critic, Lewis seemed to take delight in the role of a knight errant fighting for lost causes, defending abandoned castles, tilting at imaginary windmills. In addition to his major studies of the allegorical tradition and of the sixteenth century, two of his most provocative critical contributions are his analyses of Milton and of romanticism. In *A Preface to Paradise Lost,* a revision and enlargement of a series of lectures for university students, Lewis's stated purpose was to help modern readers appreciate the poem by revealing what Milton intended it to be. Considering the epic form to be one of the main obstacles to enjoyment of *Paradise Lost* in the twentieth century, Lewis distinguished lucidly between primary and secondary epics and analyzed in detail the stylistic features of each type. He summed up this part of the preface as a defense: "The grandeur which the poet assumes in his poetic capacity should not arouse hostile reactions. It is for our benefit. He makes his epic a rite so that we may share it; the more ritual it becomes, the more we are elevated to the rank of participants."[10] In this analogy between epic and ritual, Lewis camouflaged his provocative position by identifying himself with the readers whom he hoped to bring closer to Milton.

After a thorough and illuminating explanation of the poem's form, Lewis devoted the second half of his book to discussion of the poem's content. Admitting that his own Christianity affected his view of Milton,[11] he identified as the basic subject of *Paradise Lost* the result of disobedience in a hierarchical system. He claimed that this theme is also relevant for non-Christians, who "must just accept Milton's doctrine of obedience as they accept

the inexplicable prohibitions in *Lohengrin, Cinderella,* or
Cupid and Psyche."[12] Most readers must make "an effort of
historical imagination to evoke that whole hierarchical
conception of the universe to which Milton's poem be-
longs, and to exercise themselves in feeling as if they
believed it."[13] Lewis gave assistance in this effort by elucidating characters and situations from the viewpoint of
seventeenth-century Christian thought, with its background of Lucretius, St. Augustine, and Neo-Platonism.
But he pointed out that modern failure to appreciate
Paradise Lost involves problems wider than literary scholarship can compass. In literary terms, *Paradise Lost*

> fulfills the conditions of great story better than any
> other, it leaves things where it did not find them. . . . [It]
> records a real, irreversible, unrepeatable process in the
> history of the universe; and even for those who do not
> believe this, it embodies (in what *for them* is a mythical
> form) the great change in every individual soul. . . . The
> truth and passion of the presentation are unassailable.
> They were never, in essence, assailed until rebellion and
> pride came, in the romantic age, to be admired for their
> own sake. On this side the adverse criticism of Milton is
> not so much a literary phenomenon as the shadow cast
> upon literature by revolutionary politics, antinomian
> ethics, and the worship of Man by Man.[14]

Thus Lewis concluded his defense of Milton by affirming
that the poet's celebration of divine order illustrates the
principle of order and harmony in the universe, the
principle that distinguishes art from chaos. The artifice
and power of a dominant design link Milton with
Spenser in what Lewis saw as the great tradition of
English literature.

The reference to the shadow first cast on literature in
the romantic age involves another facet of Lewis's icon-

oclasm as a critic. He thought that Romanticism, like Renaissance, had been mistakenly revered. As an avowed romantic himself, he distinguished between two types of romanticism, one characteristic of what he considered genuine literature and the other a distortion of it. Since both types of romanticism contrasted with the neoclassicism of the eighteenth century, they are often confused. The essence of genuine romanticism, according to Lewis, is " . . . the indulgence of a *Sehnsucht* awakened by the past, the distant, and the imagined, but not believed, supernatural."[15] Lewis discovered this quality of longing in some early medieval literature, "something which, under many names, lurks at the back of most romantic poetry . . . the 'other world' not of religion, but of imagination; the land of longing, the Earthly Paradise, the garden east of the sun and west of the moon."[16] His personal belief that the world of Christian doctrine is the prototype of the world of the imagination gave added significance to this romantic longing.[17]

Lewis's definition of romanticism put the Romantic poets in a new perspective. Their significance for him was not their revolt against neoclassicism but their restoration of those features which medieval and Elizabethan poetry shared, particularly the liberation of fantasy. Yet Lewis spoke of a shadow cast on literature in the romantic age: this was not liberated fantasy's "bright shadow of reality" but the dark shadow of unrestrained instinct, the distorted facet of romanticism that he sometimes called sub-Romanticism. The rejection of discipline both in feeling and in form resulted in what Lewis considered the inartistic self-consciousness of Byron's *Childe Harold,* Joyce's *Ulysses,* or the works of D. H. Lawrence. When the imagination freed from humanist or neoclassical restraint conceived in mythic terms, the result was the great poetry of *The Faerie Queene* or *The Rime of the Ancient Mariner.*

Lewis shattered the conventional category of the Romantic. A selection, from various essays and passing references, of the literature that Lewis regarded as representative of genuine romanticism includes *Pilgrim's Progress, Gulliver's Travels, Don Juan, The Heart of Midlothian, The Egoist,* and *The Time Machine.* The catholicity of this list suggests that Lewis's definition of romantic literature may be simply what he admires; but such an oversimplification does him less than justice. He recognized the greatness of *Samson Agonistes, The Rape of the Lock, Emma, The Importance of Being Earnest,* or *The Waste Land,* all of which represent the highest artistic fusion of subject matter, poetic idea, and style, but none of which represents any aspect of romanticism. Their controlling spirit is rational, not fantastic as in genuine romanticism.

Where feeling or form are without control or restraint, Lewis identified the result as sub-Romanticism. He paid very little attention to literature in this category, but he often attacked the kind of criticism that it leads to. Lewis's insistence on myth as the essence of literature put the critical focus on the work of art itself rather than on the artist. In contrast, the sub-Romantic concept of art as free expression of the artist's personality implies that a primary function of criticism is analysis of that personality. In the case of a writer whose avowed purpose is self-expression, whose imagination is introspective, such analysis may be highly relevant; the danger of this kind of critical sub-Romanticism is its application to literature for which it is irrelevant. Discovery of some of Milton's theological heresies and personal eccentricities could lead to the assumption that they are embodied in his characterization of God, Satan, or Adam. By considering " . . . all the connections . . . in Milton's private thinking . . . you will find out many interesting facts, but you will not be able to judge or enjoy the tragedy. In *Paradise Lost* we are to study what the poet, with his singing robes about him, has given us. And when we study that we find that he has laid aside most of his private theological whimsies during his working hours as an epic poet. He may have been an undisciplined man; he was a very disciplined artist."[18] Similarly, to assume that Samson as a blind old man represents Milton as a blind old man is to miss the unifying theme of *Samson Agonistes*.[19] The imaginative creation of the character of Satan or Samson incorporates some of Milton's personal experience but is controlled by his deliberate selectivity. It is irrelevant to make deductions either about the poet's own life on the basis of his characters or about the characters on the basis of his personal experience.

Sub-Romantic criticism involves another kind of misinterpretation of literature: if the artist is expected to express conscious or unconscious personal experience, then a writer who does not do so is considered false or insincere. Lewis pointed out that Elizabethan sonnet sequences were intended not as "true confessions" but as variations on a theme, usually the theme of love. The sonneteer looked in his heart to write, "but when a poet looks in his heart he finds many things there besides the actual. That is why, and how, he is a poet."[20] Whether the feeling expressed in the work of art coincides with the artist's personal feelings is irrelevant in evaluation. Lewis defended one of his own favorite writers, Sir Walter Scott, against the possible charge of insincerity. Despite passages expressing "dark estimates of life and men" in Scott's journal, Lewis found cheerfulness predominant in his novels; this was not insincerity, but fidelity to the form of the novel as comedy (not a "comment on life"). Lewis said that Scott "usually rejected unhappy endings not because he believed, or wanted his readers to believe, or ever for a moment supposed they would believe, that irretrievable disasters never occurred in real life, but because they were inconsistent with the sort of work he was making."[21] Whether Scott's pessimism was habitual or occasional, the optimism of his work is constant. If a writer's lack of personal discipline results in distortions of form or style, then the work must be appraised on the basis of technical defects. But judgment of the conduct of, for instance, Shelley, should not prejudice the reader's appreciation of the poetry.

The sub-Romantic critic seemed to Lewis not only to misinterpret or misjudge literature but also to misuse it. Although a psychoanalyst may glean valuable information from the patient's dreams, the critic cannot use literature in the same way. Just as a work of art is not necessarily an expression of the writer's conscious experience, neither must it be a revelation of his unconscious mind. Lewis disparaged the attempt to discover what the man Shakespeare was like by analyzing the sonnets and would have been impatient with some of the studies of his own fiction. Whatever the subtle links between the writer and his work, they are irrelevant to the reader's understanding and enjoyment. According to Lewis's theory of mythopoeia, the image occurs to the writer and appeals to the reader because of its fundamental significance, its existence in the sphere of universal reality. When Lewis said that every genuinely romantic writer "builds a bridge between the conscious and the unconscious mind,"[22] he referred not to the writer's own unconscious mind but to the collective unconscious of the race.

Whatever Lewis said about writers, literary fashions, or the intellectual or spiritual climate of other periods was intended to clarify the incidental elements in literature that depend on circumstances; once these have been taken into consideration, great literature of any kind and of any period satisfies, according to Lewis, the same basic laws of the human imagination. As a result of this theory, he challenged many conventional classifications and judgments. He often seemed perverse because his arguments, however logical their form, depended on the imagination, not the reason, for their ultimate justification. And his own imaginative responses were not necessarily universal; many of his fellow Christians do not enjoy Spenser or Milton, and some of his fellow Spenserians and Miltonists are not Christians. The champion of medieval literature has not inspired as many followers as the Christian apologist has converted skeptics. Lewis's techniques in these two roles were as different as his audiences. But his ultimate purpose was the same.

In the preface to *Mere Christianity,* Lewis stated a purpose relevant to all of his religious writing: "I am not trying to convert any one to my own position. Ever since I became a Christian I have thought that the best, perhaps the only service I could do for my unbelieving neighbours was to explain and defend the belief that has been common to nearly all Christians at nearly all times."[23] As a layman converted from agnosticism, Lewis explained in clear and powerful terms the reasons for accepting basic Christian doctrine. Concentrating always on the features that unite rather than those that divide the churches, he attributed his success to the truth of the doctrine rather than to his own rhetorical skills. He was and continues to be a major influence in quickening and strengthening faith.

As a scholar and critic, Lewis used more subtle techniques for a more limited audience. Only those professionally interested in English literature are likely to have read the books discussed in this chapter, some of which originated as university lectures. Lewis was not explaining to unbelievers or defending against attackers as he was in his religious apologetics; instead, he was attacking some strongly held positions that he thought would threaten rather than secure the literary heritage. His mode of attack was indirect. He discredited the Renaissance by showing its most attractive features to be universal and its least attractive features to be most characteristic. He repudiated certain types of romanticism by suggesting that they subordinated the free play of the human psyche to the methodology of the psychoanalyst. He tried to show that many of the apparent bulwarks of literary opinion were really cardboard structures when seen from a different perspective. What he could not thus circumvent with new angles of vision, he could undermine with satiric wit. Lewis often seemed dogmatic in his criticism, attacking in order to recapture readers for the kind of literature he liked best. There was, however, an underlying purpose in Lewis's literary campaign that was not concerned with scoring academic victories over his opponents. (He would not object to the military metaphor; his favorite books and his own fiction are as full of good fights as the Bible or the classical epic.) His crusade was to reclaim the world of fantasy, that "larger, brighter, bitterer, more dangerous world than ours," and share its freehold. The gateway to this world is open to all. Lewis rallied his fellow lovers of literature in the hope that they would show the next generation the path. In disparaging the Renaissance, he was promoting another kind of *renascentia,* a rebirth of enjoyment of literature at a time when he considered imagination to be in danger of atrophy or suffocation. Thus as a scholarly critic Lewis was also a prophetic teacher.

Chapter V

THE TEACHER'S ROLE

For every one pupil who needs to be guarded from a weak excess of sensibility there are three who need to be awakened from the slumber of cold vulgarity. —THE ABOLITION OF MAN

Although C. S. Lewis said he would be remembered (if at all) as the creator of Narnia, the occupation that demanded most of his time for nearly forty years was teaching. His fellow Oxford English don and friend from student days, Nevill Coghill, called him "easily the greatest teacher of our time in his chosen fields."[1] Lewis seemed to write with an audience of undergraduates in mind, determined to keep them awake, to shock them with reconsideration of stock ideas, to challenge judgment, provoke response, and stimulate imagination. Most of Lewis's scholarly and critical books originated as university lectures, some as regular courses, others as special series. Many of his essays were published after being presented at meetings of student societies or professional associations; one collection of these is called *They Asked For a Paper,*[2] as they so often did. Even after revisions for publication, the tone of his speaking voice is predominant. When Coghill defined Lewis's critical works as "magistral,"[3] he meant authoritative, representative of a Master of his art—but he also evoked the image of the schoolmaster standing in the wings to prompt the professor.

One of the most direct examples of Lewis in his role as teacher is his advice to student writers in *Studies in Words*:

> One of the first things we have to say to a beginner who has brought us his MS. is, "Avoid all epithets which are merely emotional. It is no use *telling* us that something was "mysterious" or "loathsome" or "awe-inspiring" or "voluptuous." Do you think your readers will believe you just because you say so? You must go quite a different way to work. By direct descriptions, by metaphor and simile, by secretly evoking powerful associations, by offering the right stimuli to our nerves (in the right degree and the right order), and by the very beat and vowel-melody and length and brevity of your sentences, you must bring it about that we, we readers, not you, exclaim "how mysterious!" or "loathsome" or whatever it is. Let me taste for myself, and you'll have no need to *tell* me how I should react to the flavour."[4]

This passage is particularly interesting in comparison with a letter Lewis wrote to a child in Florida who had sent him a manuscript:

> What really matters is:
> (1) Always try to use the language so as to make quite clear what you mean, and make sure your sentence couldn't mean anything else.
> (2) Always prefer the plain direct word to the long vague one. Don't "implement" promises, but "keep" them.
> (3) Never use abstract nouns when concrete ones will do. If you mean "more people died," don't say "mortality rose."
> (4) In writing, don't use adjectives which merely tell us how you want us to feel about the thing you are

describing. I mean, instead of telling us a thing was "terrible," describe it so that we'll be terrified. Don't say it was "delightful!", make *us* say "delightful" when we've read the description. You see, all those words (horrifying, wonderful, hideous, exquisite) are only saying to your readers "Please will you do my job for me."[5]

The fourth point is exactly what he recommended to university students, but expressed in terms a child could understand. In his many letters to children, he showed the teacher's gift of communicating on their level without talking down to them. Another good example is his reply to an American schoolgirl who had written at her teacher's suggestion to ask Lewis's advice about writing:

It is very hard to give any general advice about writing. Here's my attempt.
(1) Turn off the radio.
(2) Read all the good books you can, and avoid nearly all magazines.
(3) Always write (and read) with the ear, not the eye. You shd. hear every sentence you write as if it was being read aloud or spoken. If it does not sound nice, try again.
(4) Write about what really interests you, whether it is real things or imaginary things, and nothing else. (Notice this means that if you are interested *only* in writing you will never be a writer, because you will have nothing to write about. . . .)[6]

These practical suggestions from a master to a novice show no condescension. They are principles Lewis followed himself. In attending to this young writer's needs, Lewis moderated his authoritative voice with a tone of personal interest. He had the master teacher's talent for establishing rapport with his pupils.

Lewis's popularity as a tutor at Oxford was, however, by no means unanimous. Recollections by his former students indicate that they were inspired or intimidated, but never bored, by him. In "The Tutor and the Scholar" John Lawlor describes how his reaction changed from hostility to affection and gratitude as he began to realize the purpose in Lewis's impersonal and argumentative stance.[7] When Lawlor asked for a paper to inaugurate a student English society, Lewis obliged with "Our English Syllabus," in which he spoke of the student's role in terms that implied a concept of the teacher's role: "The student is, or ought to be, a young man who is already beginning to follow learning for its own sake, and who attaches himself to an older student, not precisely to be taught, but to pick up what he can."[8] Lawlor considers that this passage conveys the spirit of Lewis's tutoring; its suggestion of the medieval university or the Greek academy is typical of Lewis. In putting the responsibility on the student, he challenged some and bewildered others. Lawlor points out that it was not necessarily the best students who liked him best; some with brilliant minds were ill at ease in his tutorials.

The impressions vary to the point of contradiction. In the collective biography, *The Inklings,* Humphrey Carpenter suggests that Lewis was successful with only a minority: "A few managed to fight back and even win a point—which was just what Lewis wanted them to do— but the majority were cowed by the force of his dialectic and went away abashed."[9] In another context Carpenter, who was at Oxford himself and knew Tolkien but not Lewis, reduces "the majority" to numbers more nearly equal to those of the enthusiastic: "For every one of them who (like John Wain) managed to enjoy and to ape

Lewis's forceful logic, there were at least as many who were alarmed and cowed by the heavy-handedness of his manner, combined with his general refusal to put his relationship with his pupils on anything like a personal footing. A few lapped it up, but some very nearly ran away."[10]

Even among those who enjoyed Lewis's demanding tutorial style, there are contradictions as to whether Lewis really enjoyed teaching. Derek Brewer (Master of Emmanuel College, Cambridge, and Chaucerian scholar), like John Wain (critic and novelist) and Roger Lancelyn Green (Lewis's biographer), was a pupil who followed Lewis's profession and remained his friend. He insists that Lewis disliked teaching: "How pleased one would be, he remarked at the end of a tutorial, . . . if one met a man with whom one could pass an hour talking about literature; yet what a bore tutorials are doing the same thing! . . . There was perhaps something sharp and schoolmasterly about his lectures, deriving from his conviction, energy, and clarity of mind, not from any desire to dominate. He despised teaching."[11] Brewer's memoir, with twenty-two others, appears in C. S. Lewis at the Breakfast Table; the allusion in this title is not borne out by the contents. Lewis was no autocrat. Brewer's suggestion that he despised teaching *because* he had no desire to dominate must be considered in relation to John Wain's emphasis on his humility as a teacher. Wain's essay in the collection ends with Chaucer's praise of the Oxford scholar as an epitaph for Lewis: "gladly wolde he lerne and gladly teche."[12] Wain confirmed this impression in his tribute to Lewis in *The American Scholar*, the first in a series on great teachers; he explained Lewis's objections to the attitudes of some of his colleagues and students, but he stressed Lewis's relish for his profession. Wain's concluding praise echoes Chaucer: "I am glad to have been his pupil."[13] If Lewis was ever bored with tutorials, that may have been because some students were not really glad to learn and merely wanted to pass examinations. Or he may have hated the thought that his pupils would learn and repeat what he said instead of experiencing for themselves the joy in literature that he wanted to share.

There was apparently no controversy about Lewis's popularity and preeminence as a lecturer. Green affirms: "It was obvious . . . that one was listening not merely to a scholar of immense erudition, but to a lover of literature who had read every text he mentioned, had enjoyed most of them, and was eager to share his knowledge and his enthusiasm with anyone whom he could persuade to do so."[14] However disputatious and provocative he may have been in tutorials, in lectures he was always persuasive. His techniques of persuasion were not those of a man who disliked teaching or scorned his students; the operative word is "share." The poet Kathleen Raine, who met Lewis during his last years at Cambridge, found that ". . . for him learning was a joyful and inexhaustible game. Among so many academic figures whose attitude towards literature was one of bored superiority or active hatred, his love of the material itself was life-giving as a spring in a desert. I went to some of his lectures on the 'matter' of Rome, France, and Britain, and remember how he made the dullest Latin text seem enthralling (he would I am sure here have retorted that no one could possibly consider Boethius dull). The element of play was never very far away."[15] To say that he approached learning and teaching as if he were playing a game does not, of course, imply that he was not serious. Like the best professionals—or the best artisans, for that matter—he seemed to find his work delight, not drudgery.

Lewis's ideas about teaching were not influenced by current theories of education. His were the methods of Socrates and of Jesus. He gave credit in *Surprised By Joy* to two teachers who had shaped his early life most: the classics master who was one of the few redeeming features of his detested boarding school, and the retired headmaster who tutored him privately for his Oxford scholarship examinations. Of the first, Harry Wakelyn Smith, he said: "He could enchant but he could also analyze. . . . He made us feel that the scholar's demand for accuracy was not merely pedantic, still less an arbitrary moral discipline, but rather a niceness, a delicacy. . . . I began to see that the reader who misses syntactical points in a poem is missing aesthetic points as well."[16] The second of these teachers, William T. Kirkpatrick, concentrated on analysis rather than on aesthetics or enchantment. He challenged every statement, insisted on getting back to first principles, trained his pupil in definition of terms and logical argument. The description of their sessions sounds very much like Lewis's own students' accounts of tutorials. The old rationalist's most encouraging response "meant that your remark was significant and only required refutation; it had risen to the dignity of error."[17] This was the training that helped Lewis to develop what he called "intellectual muscle." He felt a great debt to this dialectician, whom he called "the Great Knock."

While Lewis emulated the adversarial logician in tutorials, in lectures he apparently had in mind also the example of the classicist: "a permanent reminder of things more gracious, more humane, larger and cooler."[18] Traits of both are reflected in a letter to an undergraduate assigned to him for tutoring in political thought (which he taught in addition to English). He sent the new pupil a detailed advance reading list, written out in longhand, with characteristically helpful comments. Its final paragraph combines the manner of Smith with the method of Kirkpatrick: "The subject, after a little reading, can be practised all day long. Start from your own political views and regard every theory either as a welcome ally or an enemy you'll have to circumvent (that makes you remember them). When you hear people arguing politics, *listen,* and try to see what theories are unconsciously implied in their remarks ('that fellow is a pure Aristotelian though he doesn't know it')."[19] The suggestion that the student will remember ideas by considering them as welcome allies or as enemies is a clue to basic features of his pedagogical strategy. He incited students to think, to make judgments—above all, to care.

Lewis's concept of the teacher's role is embodied in such important characters as Dr. Dimble in *That Hideous Strength,* the Professor in *The Lion, the Witch and the Wardrobe,* and the Fox in *Till We Have Faces.* Whether or not they reveal facets of the author himself, they clearly illustrate the strengths and the limitations of the good teacher.

The enemies of traditional civilization in *That Hideous Strength* did not consider the English professor a threat to their plans: "'Except that he's a Christian, there isn't really much against him. He's purely academic. I shouldn't think his name is much known, except to other scholars in his own subject. Not the kind that would make a public man. Impractical. . . . he'd be too full of scruples to be much use to them.'"[20] The passage is ironic because the reader already knows that this mild-mannered don is an expert on Arthurian legend, first mentioned in the novel as a matter apparently of academic interest only. Another side of the professor's role is revealed when Dimble uses his argumentative powers in a confrontation with the young sociologist recruited by the threatening research institute.[21] However, when the crisis comes, the professor's logic is useless; only Dimble's knowledge of the Great Tongue[22] makes possible an appeal to the powers of Deep Heaven for help. After the rescue of England from the forces of evil, the leader of the small victorious group leaves it to Dimble to explain the significance of what has happened and what *may* happen.[23] The professor emphasizes that no one knows what or where the next conflict between good and evil will be. He does not claim to have all the answers; he merely shows his friends what the vital questions should be.

Another professor figures less in the story but equally in the theme of *The Lion, The Witch and the Wardrobe*. When the two older children are concerned about Lucy's incredible tale of an enchanted land reached through the wardrobe in the spare room, they decide to consult the old professor to whose house they have been evacuated from wartime London. After receiving them courteously and listening to their account without interrupting, the Professor startles Peter and Susan by suggesting that Lucy's story could be true:

"Logic!" said the Professor half to himself. "Why don't they teach logic at these schools? There are only three possibilities. Either your sister is telling lies, or she is mad, or she is telling the truth. You know she doesn't tell lies and it is obvious that she is not mad. For the moment then and unless any further evidence turns up, we must assume that she is telling the truth."

Susan looked at him very hard and was quite sure from the expression on his face that he was not making fun of them.[24]

When the children point out that they saw nothing in the wardrobe and that no time elapsed during Lucy's adventure, the Professor has a ready explanation:

> "That is the very thing that makes her story so likely to be true," said the Professor. "If there really is a door in this house that leads to some other world . . . I should not be at all surprised to find that that other world had a separate time of its own. . . . "
>
> "But do you really mean, Sir," said Peter, "that there could be other worlds—all over the place, just round the corner—like that?"
>
> "Nothing is more probable," said the Professor, taking off his spectacles and beginning to polish them, while he muttered to himself, "I wonder what they *do* teach them at these schools."[25]

Here the Professor treats the children exactly as Lewis treated undergraduates, startling and confusing them with unexpected questions, leading them to think out issues for themselves, cutting them off abruptly. In this process he establishes not only some basic principles of logic but also some basic principles about the relativity of our concepts of space and time. When after many years in Narnia the children return to the wardrobe at the same time they entered it to hide, the Professor (unlike most adults) believes their story and gives them some advice:

> "Yes, of course you'll get back to Narnia again some day. Once a king in Narnia, always a King in Narnia. But don't go trying to use the same route twice. . . . And don't mention it to anyone else unless you find that they've had adventures of the same sort themselves. . . .

How will you know? . . . Keep your eyes open. Bless me, what *do* they teach them at these schools?"

And that is the very end of the adventures of the wardrobe. But if the Professor was right it was only the beginning of the adventures of Narnia.[26]

Thus the story closes on two thematic notes characteristic of Lewis: while affirming the paradox that the end may be a beginning, he reminds us that even the professor's knowledge is open to question.

The most complex of Lewis's fictional teachers is the Fox, Greek slave tutor to the barbarian princesses in *Till We Have Faces*. His significance is first intimated when the narrator, the eldest sister, mentions him three times in the first two pages. Finally she describes him and his role:

> . . . he did not look like any other slave we had ever known. He was very bright-eyed, and whatever of his hair and beard was not grey was reddish.
>
> "Now, Greekling," said my father to this man, "I trust to beget a prince one of these days and I have a mind to see him brought up in all the wisdom of your people. Meanwhile practice on *them*." (He pointed at us children.) "If a man can teach a girl, he can teach anything." Then, just before he sent us away, he said, "Especially the elder. See if you can make her wise; it's about all she'll ever be good for."[27]

His last remark is typical of the king's scorn for his ugly daughter, which contrasts with the Fox's appreciation of her intelligence.

The nickname based on the Fox's bright eyes and reddish-gray hair also suggests his shrewdness, which is featured later in the novel in his advice to Orual as queen. In the early chapters, the emphasis is on the qualities that contribute most to the young girl's education. The first point she makes is that she loves him, admiring his cheerfulness, which is sustained even in slavery by his inquisitiveness. He is always as eager to learn as to teach. His most specific link with Socrates is his insistence that the wonderful Greek stories he tells her are "'only lies of poets, lies of poets, child. Not in accordance with nature'" (p. 8). He says the same about the local superstition that a certain wood used for the royal bed would cause four out of five children begotten there to be male: "'All folly, child, . . . these things come about by natural causes'" (p. 10). Orual senses the difference between the two kinds of lies and perceives the limitations of the Fox's rationalism: "It was always like that with the Fox; he was ashamed of loving poetry ('All folly, child') and I had to work much at my reading and writing and what he called philosophy in order to get a poem out of him. But thus, little by little, he taught me many" (p. 8). The pupil's response to the Fox's instinctive love of poetry overcomes his Greek principles of education. However, the king sees his educated slave merely as a tool to further his own ends. He insists that the Fox teach the princesses and a chorus of noble girls to sing a Greek hymn for his second marriage: "'Teach 'em, Fox, teach 'em,' roared my father. 'What's the use of my spending good food and drink on your Greek belly if I'm not to get a Greek song out of you on my wedding night? . . . No one's asking you to teach them Greek. Of course they won't understand what they're singing, but they can make the noises. See to it, or your back'll be redder than ever your beard was'" (pp. 10–11).

The Fox is threatened with demotion when the second marriage produces only another daughter rather than a son to be educated, but he is saved because the king needs his ability as a sophist: "The Fox was a true Greek;

where my father could give only a Yes or a No to some neighbouring king or dangerous noble, he could pare the Yes to the very quick and sweeten the No till it went down like wine. He could make your weak enemy believe you were his best friend and make your strong enemy believe you were twice as strong as you really were. He was far too useful to be sent to the mines" (pp. 19–20). This shrewd rhetorical skill is incidental in the novel, as it is superficial in the Fox; his reason and his kindness are the qualities that influence Orual. Although the Fox sometimes despairs of ever "washing the nurse and the grandam and the priest and the soothsayer" out of her soul (p. 143), he is responsible for her development as a queen whose rule over Glome is much more like the Greek ideal of justice than like her father's barbarian exploitation of power. One of her first royal decrees is to free the Fox himself; then she must use the powers of persuasion he has taught her to keep him as her counselor (pp. 207–10).

Wise as he is, the Fox is a teacher whose Greek philosophy is inadequate for the ultimate questions. After he persuades the new young priest to replace the ugly stone image of the fertility goddess, Ungit, with a beautiful statue ordered from Greece, Orual learns from a peasant woman that the common people prefer the old, shapeless, bloody stone: "'That other, the Greek Ungit, she wouldn't understand my speech. She's only for nobles and learned men. There's no comfort in her'" (p. 272). As the young priest applies the Fox's teaching, the temple becomes more sanitary but less holy. The Fox acknowledges that there are mysteries he cannot fathom. When Orual discusses with him her beloved sister Psyche's evident delusion about her bridegroom, he explains in psychological terms the cause which, he says, "'. . . needs no Oedipus.

But the real riddle's still to guess. What must we do? Oh, I'm barren, barren'" (p. 144).

Ultimately Orual herself finds the answer through a vision, in which the Fox fulfils the role of her guide. He shows her murals that depict her own human relationships so clearly that she understands fully, for the first time, both herself and Psyche. What the Fox never understands in life, the Fox in her vision explains: "' . . . even I, who am dead, do not understand more than a few broken words of their [the gods'] language. Only this I know. This age of ours will one day be the distant past. And the Divine Nature can change the past. Nothing is yet in its true form'" (p. 305). Thus the pupil, who through revelation has gone beyond her tutor, still attributes her perception to the teaching that first developed her mind and her imagination.

In the relationship between Orual and her teacher, Lewis revealed the aims of liberal education. While almost everything he wrote has some direct or indirect reference to his concern with education ("'What *do* they teach them in these schools?'"), the most specific statement is in *The Abolition of Man*. This brief but important book is the text of three lectures given at Durham University in 1943 and addressed to teachers of English. During the war, when the obvious external threat to humanity was Fascism, Lewis pointed out a subtle internal danger whose far-reaching effects he feared. It is typical of his style and method that he focused on a specific example; like Socrates asking his friends to think of the maker of beds or the tamer of horses, like Jesus telling his hearers to consider the lilies of the field or the man on the road to Jericho, Lewis always particularized. The use of specific example, of analogy and metaphor, often left him vulnerable to the charge of oversimplification. In this case the limitation of focus was not merely rhetorical; he based his warning about the potential "abolition of man" on one specific textbook as an example of a trend.

American as well as English teachers and students became familiar with the type during the 1940s and 50s. Designed for the upper forms of English secondary schools, the book was on the level of an American high-school senior or college freshman English course. Its aim was to improve critical reading and clear exposition by concentrating on logical analysis and the connotations of words. There were sections dealing with logical fallacies and rhetorical manipulation in commercial advertising, in political propaganda, and in the news media. Although Lewis did not cite the authors or title of the text, he insisted that it was actual, not hypothetical, and that he had a copy on his shelves. He described its contents in enough detail for any English teacher to recognize similar texts on his own shelves.

Lewis did not discount the importance of the kind of discrimination urged by the authors. *That Hideous Strength* illustrates the dangers of mass communication as used by the Institute, which is committed to genetic reorganization and social conditioning of the population along lines suggestive of *Brave New World* or *A Clockwork Orange.* The first act of positive evil demanded of the young sociologist recruit is to write two newspaper editorials about a violent demonstration engineered by Institute agents; in order to make the morning editions, he must write them in advance. Lewis's parody of the styles of a high-brow paper and a low-brow paper are so close to actual editorials as to be frightening.[28] Here, as in many parts of this novel, the reader recognizes that Lewis's flair for satire was at least equal to his gift for fantasy. It is clear that he recognized the necessity of critical reading, of careful analysis.

What Lewis disputed in the textbook were the assumptions implicit in such analysis: while challenging rhetorical appeals to the emotions as subjective, the authors suggested that all appeals to emotion are suspect; in rejecting the sophists' attempts to make the worse appear the better cause, they repudiated the tragic dramatists as well; in identifying underlying prejudice and bias in argument, they implied that there are no absolutes, no first principles, no universal truths. Lewis warned that if all value judgments are disparaged as being merely subjective, there are two potential dangers: the values inherited from man's past will be lost, and man will be vulnerable to any power that tries to condition and control him. Lewis feared that under the guise of freeing minds for independent thinking, such teaching would impair the emotional and imaginative faculties necessary for the comprehension of real truth. There are some truths deep in the human conscious or unconscious mind that are not subject to analysis: "It is no use trying to 'see through' first principles. If you see through everything, then everything is transparent. But a wholly transparent world is an invisible world. To 'see through' all things is the same as not to see."[29] Logical analysis and emotional response must be integrated, not segregated.

Lewis believed that the responsibility of any teacher, particularly the teacher of literature, is to nourish the responsive and imaginative faculties. Such teaching can be branded as conditioning of a different kind. But the difference is important: while the behaviorist conditions man's animal nature, the basic assumption of imaginative literature is that man's nature is more than animal. Made in the image of his Maker, man has the power to perceive the Creator through the creation and, in turn, to share his perceptions with other human beings by making his own images. This fundamental conviction, central to Lewis's own imaginative and critical writing, should be a basic premise for the teacher of literature.

Lewis's theories of myth as the essence of literature, and of metaphor as the basic mode of language, as discussed above in Chapters II and III, imply that appreciation of literature does not have to be imposed on anyone; the capacity is inherent and must instead be nourished, cultivated, developed. The original Latinate definition of *education* as "leading out" is the relevant one for Lewis's concept of what the teacher should do. He feared that teaching which concentrated on facts and logic to the exclusion of fantasy would cause atrophy of the imaginative faculties. The question raised by the Professor in *The Lion, the Witch and the Wardrobe* about what they teach in schools is answered in *The Voyage of the Dawn Treader,* with the introduction of Eustace Clarence Scrubb: "Eustace Clarence liked animals, especially beetles, if they were dead and pinned on a card. He liked books if they were books of information and had pictures of grain elevators or of fat foreign children doing exercises in model schools."[30] Surely Lewis meant that pictures of foreign countries should portray something unusual and fascinating about them rather than illustrate what propagandists have identified as progress: the Great Wall of China or the golden domes of Samarkand, rather than mass calisthenics for Communist youth. The main point becomes clear later in the story when Eustace takes refuge in a cave where he cannot get his bearings: "Most of us know what we should expect to find in a dragon's lair, but, as I said before, Eustace had read only the wrong books. They had a lot to say about exports and imports and governments and drains, but they were weak on dragons."[31] Eustace had been given the wrong books not only by his parents but by the teachers at his "progressive" school, which is described in the first chapter of the next Narnia chronicle, *The Silver Chair*. Eustace must learn about dragons painfully, through personal experience, because his education has not prepared him for that kind of reality. He has been cheated of part of his cultural inheritance. This danger is what Lewis warned would bring about "the abolition of man," the loss of basic human values. One aim of education is to transmit those values.

A different aspect of the aim of education is emphasized in *An Experiment in Criticism*. Instead of presenting students with material predigested for their assimilation, the teacher should direct them to the raw ingredients, show them the basic techniques of following recipes, and then let them experiment and taste for themselves. This extended culinary metaphor derives from Lewis's frequent use of "taste" in both its physical and its literary senses. A master chef could judge that a particular dish was well made, but only the individual diner could judge whether it tasted good to him; similarly, a scholar or critic can label a literary work in terms of its fidelity to a particular form, but only the reader can say whether or not he is moved by it. The function of the teacher is to give the reader information and experience as background for his development of personal taste. From this point of view, Lewis stressed the traditional curriculum of languages, history, philosophy, and the Bible as essential. He did not believe that pupils of any age should be allowed to do just what they pleased. (This is one of the mistakes made at Eustace's school.) They must acquire knowledge in the field (and his idea applies in varying ways to all fields of knowledge), but this knowledge should always be seen as a means to an end, not as an end in itself. The end for literary studies is the pleasure of reading good books.

With this criterion, Lewis distinguished three groups of readers: the mere professionals, who know a great deal about literature but are often bored by what they read; the status seekers or devotees of culture; and those who read for the love of it. While followers of fashion "drop the Georgians and begin to admire Mr. Eliot, acknowledge the 'dislodgement' of Milton, and discover Hopkins, . . . the only real literary experience in such a family may be occurring in a back bedroom where a small boy is reading *Treasure Island* under the bedclothes by the light of an electric torch."[32] The distinction led him to attempt the experiment of evaluating books on the basis of how they are read. The implication of such an evaluation is that the teacher's job is not to tell students why certain books are good but to help students become good readers.

The first step in the experiment was to identify two different types of reading: using and receiving. The "user" approaches literature as a means to some end of his own, whereas the "receiver" opens himself, his mind and imagination, to receive what the author intended. Lewis characterized the user's purposes as "pastime for a dull or torturing hour, as puzzle, as a help to castle-building, or perhaps as a source for 'philosophies of life.'"[33] Instead of making fullest use of the author's style, of the rich associations of his imagery, the "user" skims only from the surface of the work. In contrast, the "receiver" finds in the style "exquisitely detailed compulsions on a mind willing and able to be so compelled."[34] For both users and receivers, reading may involve excitement, curiosity, vicarious happiness, or escapism; but the receiver will appreciate books that make too many demands on the attention of the user: "It has been maintained that the attraction of Trollope or even Jane

Austen for many readers is the imaginative truancy into an age when their class, or the class they identify with theirs, was more secure and fortunate than now. Perhaps it is sometimes so with Henry James. . . . But it can only be an initial attraction. No one who chiefly or even very strongly wants egoistic castle-building will persevere long with James, Jane Austen, or Trollope."[35] The user, according to Lewis, is a bad reader, perhaps a highly intelligent person but unliterary. The receiver is a good reader, possibly young or untrained in criticism but essentially literary.

The purpose of Lewis's experiment was to judge books in terms of readers rather than the other way round. "Let us try to discover how far it might be plausible to define a good book as a book which is read in one way, and a bad book as a book which is read in another."[36] Lewis had suggested over twenty years earlier that the generalizations about good and bad books should be discarded in favor of more valid distinctions. In an essay called "High and Low Brows" he classified low-brow books that give deep and lasting pleasure as good bad books: for instance, Rider Haggard's *She* (which Lewis preferred to *King Solomon's Mines*), or many science fiction stories.[37] In contrast, he identified bad good books that may be part of the canon of English Literature but are never read voluntarily or with delight: for example, Lyly's *Euphues*, which he called "a monstrosity," "odious," and "intolerable."[38] In the critical experiment Lewis abandoned any association of "bad" with "low-brow" or "good" with "high-brow" and concentrated entirely on the kind of readers a book attracts and the kind of reading it calls for. He repeated an old question with a rearrangement of priorities. The genuine critical question "Why and how should we read this?" was reduced to "How should we read this?"

Ideally, we must receive it first and then evaluate it. Otherwise we have nothing to evaluate. Unfortunately this idea is progressively less and less realised the longer we live in a literary profession or in literary circles. It occurs, magnificently, in young readers. At a first reading of some great work, they are "knocked flat." Criticize it? No, by God, but read it again. The judgement "This must be a great work" may be long delayed.[39]

Although the experiment focused on readers and reading rather than on teachers, it depicted Lewis's own teaching and his message for his colleagues so clearly that the book should be required for all education-majors specializing in elementary grades, in reading, or in English. The book is specifically addressed to teachers who prepare candidates for entrance to the English universities where they themselves were educated. The closest American equivalent would be teachers of Advanced Placement classes in high schools, but the point applies to a wide range of classroom reading situations. Good reading requires

> . . . that inner silence, that emptying out of ourselves, by which we ought to make room for the total reception of the work. . . .
>
> For this reason I am very doubtful whether criticism is a proper exercise for boys and girls. . . . Especially poisonous is the kind of teaching which encourages them to approach every literary work with suspicion. It springs from a very reasonable motive. In a world full of sophistry and propaganda, we want to protect the rising generation from being deceived, to forearm them against the invitations to false sentiment and muddled thinking which printed words will so often offer them. Unfortunately, the very same habit which makes them impervious to the bad writing may make them impervious also

to the good. . . . We must risk being taken in, if we are to get anything. The best safeguard against bad literature is a full experience of good.[40]

That full experience of good literature is what the teacher should make available.

After developing the entire experiment in terms of *how* books should be read, Lewis turned in an "Epilogue" to the complementary question "Why?" The answer that we should read for enjoyment as an end in itself is true but inadequate, because a work of literary art has two aspects which cause different kinds of pleasure. "It both *means* and *is*. It is both *Logos* (something said) and *Poiema* (something made). As Logos it tells a story, or expresses an emotion, or exhorts or pleads or describes or rebukes or excites laughter. As Poiema, by its aural beauties and also by the balance and contrast and the unified multiplicity of its successive parts, it is an *objet d'art*, a thing shaped so as to give great satisfaction."[41] This distinction leads to a restatement of the question and a tentative answer:

> The mark of strictly literary reading, as opposed to scientific or otherwise informative reading, is that we need not believe or approve the Logos. . . . What then is the good of—what is even the defence for—occupying our hearts with stories of what never happened and entering vicariously into feelings which we should try to avoid having in our own person? Or of fixing our inner eye earnestly on things that can never exist—on Dante's earthly paradise, Thetis rising from the sea to comfort Achilles, Chaucer's or Spenser's Lady Nature, or the Mariner's skeleton ship?
>
> It is no use trying to evade the question by locating the whole goodness of a literary work in its character as

Poiema, for it is out of our various interests in the Logos that the Poiema is made.

The nearest I have yet got to an answer is that we seek an enlargement of our being. We want to be more than ourselves.[42]

Here Lewis answers the question with a characteristic blending of conviction and diffidence. The next four pages develop this theme with variations like prose music.

The final passage of the book's coda, affirming the ultimate value of literary experience, applies also to what Lewis thought the educational experience should be: "Literary experience heals the wound, without undermining the privilege, of individuality. There are mass emotions which heal the wound; but they destroy the privilege. In them our separate selves are pooled and we sink back into sub-individuality. But in reading great literature I become a thousand men and yet remain myself. Like the night sky in the Greek poem, I see with a myriad eyes, but it is still I who see. Here, as in worship, in love, in moral action, and in knowing, I transcend myself; and am never more myself than when I do."[43] This is the experience that the good teacher hopes his students will share: the paradoxical losing and finding of the self that comes from *knowing*. And for Lewis, as for Socrates, the greatest wisdom was knowing that I do not know.

Chapter VI

THE PEDAGOGICAL STYLE

> *. . . the surprise works as well the*
> *twentieth time as the first. It is the*
> quality *of unexpectedness, not the*
> fact *that delights us.* —"ON STORIES"

The paradox at the core of Lewis's teaching was his radical approach to traditional values. He used shock tactics not merely to startle students out of their apathy and make them think for themselves—at a deeper level, he was trying in his literary as well as in his religious writing to encourage regenerative experience. In his criticism Lewis often appeared dogmatic; sometimes he sounded like one of the types he disliked most: a bully, a know-it-all, a show-off. However, a careful look at such passages reveals that he was using conventional pedagogical techniques in unconventional ways. He could have been describing his own style when he referred with relish to "the 'aged and great' dons—crusty, fruity, 'humourists' (in the old sense), fathomlessly learned, and amidst all their kindness (there's no perfect dish without some sharpness) merciless leg pullers."[1]

A fundamental principle of all teaching is to begin with what is familiar and lead the student gradually to what is unfamiliar, new, or strange. One of the best examples of Lewis's application of this principle is found

in *A Preface to Paradise Lost.* The introductory paragraph
follows a pattern typical of textbooks at many levels:

> The first qualification for judging any piece of work-
> manship from a corkscrew to a cathedral is to know *what
> it is*—what it was intended to do and how it is meant to
> be used. After that has been discovered the temperance
> reformer may decide that the corkscrew was made for a
> bad purpose, and the communist may think the same
> about the cathedral. But such questions come later. The
> first thing is to understand the object before you: as long
> as you think the corkscrew was meant for opening tins or
> the cathedral for entertaining tourists you can say noth-
> ing to the purpose about them. The first thing the
> reader needs to know about *Paradise Lost* is what Milton
> meant it to be.[2]

Anyone can understand the point about corkscrews and
cathedrals and can therefore acknowledge the necessity
of a detailed analysis of the form of epic poetry. The
illustrations were chosen for their familiarity on more
than one level. The incongruous juxtaposition of "corkscrew" and "cathedral," reinforced by alliteration, suggests a contrast between gadgetry and pageantry,
between frivolity and formality. The implied appreciation of the true purpose of both corkscrew and cathedral
relegates those who do not care about understanding
Milton to the ranks of temperance reformers or commu-
nists, inept cooks or gaping tourists. The connotations
here are as thoroughly familiar as those in a magazine
advertisement; by this focus on the familiar, Lewis not
only met the student on common ground but began
immediately to direct his route.

At the beginning of his first scholarly book, *The Allegory of Love,* Lewis met his audience on their own ground
in order to establish the necessity of two chapters of

background before the main topic. Recognizing that contemporary taste in erotic literature preferred explicit sex and equality in personal relationships, he understood why the study of medieval allegorical love poetry might seem to be useless pedantry; but he justified it in contemporary terms:

> Humanity does not pass through phases as a train passes through stations: being alive, it has the privilege of always moving yet never leaving anything behind. Whatever we have been, in some sort we are still. Neither the form nor the sentiment of this old poetry has passed away without leaving indelible traces on our minds. We shall understand our present, and perhaps even our future, the better if we can succeed, by an effort of the historical imagination, in reconstructing that long-lost state of mind for which the allegorical love poem was a natural mode of expression.[3]

Acknowledging that readers of the 1930s might be put off by both form and content, Lewis began to establish their confidence with this recognition. Reviewing this early work in the light of all of Lewis's criticism, the reader of the 1980s notices themes that Lewis was to develop fully elsewhere. The familiar distinction between popular and intellectual literature was one of his frequent targets. Preference for Lawrence, Forster, or Woolf did not seem to Lewis necessarily more sophisticated or mature, merely more "modern" or "contemporary." Thus Lewis suggested that the point where the reader stood was not necessarily as advantageous as the one to which the argument was leading. Lewis aroused a demand for more knowledge.

The longer he taught, the more Lewis seemed to realize the limitations of his readers' starting point. In *The Allegory of Love* he assumed more familiarity with classical literature than he did in *The Discarded Image*, published nearly thirty years later. During the intervening generation, study of the classics had declined in England and had nearly died in the United States. Even students of English literature at Oxford and Cambridge lacked the classical background necessary for understanding medieval literature; they found Lewis's lectures so valuable that some of them urged him to give a more permanent form to his lecture notes. He prefaced the resulting book with a justification for detailed analysis of the medieval Model of the Universe as it figured in literature. He hoped that his explanations would enable students to read and enjoy the books without constantly consulting the notes: "To be always looking at the map when there is a fine prospect before you shatters the 'wise passiveness' in which landscape ought to be enjoyed. But to consult a map before we set out has no such ill effect. Indeed it will lead us to many prospects; including some we might never have found by following our noses."[4] But the analogy between literature and landscape is oversimplified. Another analogy suggests the more complex experience of reading:

> There are, I know, those who prefer not to go beyond the impression, however accidental, which an old work makes on a mind that brings to it a purely modern sensibility and modern conceptions; just as there are travellers who carry their resolute Englishry with them all over the Continent, mix only with other English tourists, enjoy all they see for its "quaintness," and have no wish to realise what those ways of life, those churches, those vineyards, mean to the natives. They have their reward. I have no quarrel with people who approach the past in that spirit. I hope they will pick none with me. But I was writing for the other sort.[5]

Any reader who identifies himself with "the other sort" of perceptive tourist is ready to set out with Lewis as guide. The reader who recognizes the Biblical allusion (Matthew 6: 2, 5, 16) is likely to realize what direction the guide will take.

One of the most characteristic features of Lewis's style is the sudden introduction of commonplace, present-day illustrations for complex or remote points. In describing the way the ideals of courtly love had permeated society, he said: "To leap up on errands, to go through heat or cold, at the bidding of one's lady, or even of any lady, would seem but honourable and natural to a gentleman of the thirteenth or even of the seventeenth century; and most of us have gone shopping in the twentieth with ladies who showed no sign of regarding the tradition as a dead letter."[6] Even more familiar is the analogy used to excuse a late medieval poet for his apparent delight in fitting a list of names into a complex stanzaic pattern: "One may call such ingenuity perverse, but one must not call it affected—unless the very young cyclist is affected when he first revels in the discovery that he can ride with his hands off the handle bars."[7]

Sometimes Lewis developed these familiar, contemporary illustrations in more detail, as in his character sketch of Pandarus from Chaucer's *Troilus and Criseyde*: "Every one has met the modern equivalent of Pandarus. When you are in the hands of such a man you can travel first class through the length and breadth of England on a third-class ticket; policemen and game-keepers will fade away before you, placated yet unbribed; noble first-floor bedrooms will open for you in hotels that have sworn they are absolutely full; and drinks will be forthcoming at hours when the rest of the world goes thirsty."[8] This comparison is a comment on modern society as well as on

Pandarus. The type is familiar, the illustration vivid, the implication teasing.

Lewis's commonplace details may be metaphoric rather than illustrative, as in his comment on Kipling's meticulous revisions of his stories: "His work was meant to be taken in small doses. The man who gobbles down one story after another at a sitting has no more right to complain if the result is disastrous than the man who swills liqueurs as if they were beer."[9] The metaphor is characteristic in that it relates to eating and drinking; nothing could be more basic, more certainly experience shared by all his audience. In describing his occasional feeling of strong distaste for Kipling, Lewis referred to "the difference between feeling that, on the whole, you would not like another slice of bread and butter just now and wondering, as your gorge rises, how you could ever have imagined that you like vodka."[10]

Usually the food and drink imagery is positive rather than negative. Lewis expressed his relish for the argumentative style of the Knock's teaching by calling it "red meat and strong beer."[11] Recognizing that tastes vary, he praised an Elizabethan writer who "offers sweets in plenty for the young and amorous reader," as well as "solid nourishment for maturer stomachs."[12] The idea of intellectual or spiritual "nourishment" is such a commonplace that it has almost lost its figurative sense, but reference to "stomachs" confirms the metaphor. Not at all commonplace is Lewis's description of the historical material in Holinshed's *Chronicles* as "a sort of national stock-pot permanently simmering to which each new cook adds flavouring at his discretion."[13] In addition to separate metaphors like these, the imagery of taste can be a leitmotif. In *English Literature in the Sixteenth Century*, the Golden poetry is frequently described as honey, and the literary achievements of the century are summed up in the same figure: "We stole most of the honey which the humanists were carrying without suffering very much from their stings."[14] Throughout *A Preface to Paradise Lost*, the seventeenth-century preference for decorum and ceremony is explained in terms of a feast or a dinner party. A similar metaphor is used to illustrate the original readers' demand for Milton's poetic diction: they wanted poetry to "be *familiar* in the sense of being expected [but] not be *familiar* in the sense of being colloquial and commonplace. A parallel, from a different sphere, would be turkey and plum pudding on Christmas day; no one is surprised at the menu, but every one recognizes that it is not *ordinary* fare."[15] The suggestion that "no one is surprised" and "every one recognizes" is basic to Lewis's teaching techinque. He always made his readers feel at ease, with a range of imagery based on commonplace details.

After introducing the unfamiliar in terms of the familiar, Lewis used other pedagogical techniques to reach his audience. One such technique was the organization of material into categories or compartments, often with distinctive and memorable labels. Every teacher realizes that categories and labels tend to oversimplify material, but they are useful to save time, to get the essentials on the blackboard, to help students organize their notes and focus their learning. Categories and labels are merely a convenience, not models for truth. Lewis's most characteristic use of them was for the purpose of redirecting attention, tearing down watertight compartments, and making his readers reconsider conventional judgments. In his lecture about "High and Low Brows," he suggested a sweeping reclassification of literature. Attacking the conventional critic's or teacher's classification of "high-brow" books as "good" and "low-brow" books as "bad," he put many dull, unread, and unreadable works from the English syllabus into the "bad" category and much widely beloved light reading into the "good"[16]—but his choices for these categories were illustrative, not definitive. He wanted each reader to make his own choices. The colloquial connotations of the terms "high-brow" and "low-brow" mocked the whole concept of arbitrary classification.

Lewis used classification as a technique to challenge classification in one of his last books, *An Experiment in Criticism*. The experiment was to reclassify books on the basis of the kind of reading that they evoke, or the kind of reader who enjoys them. Replacing the category "good book" with that of "good reader," Lewis identified four main features of the good reader: (1) frequent rereading of favorites; (2) giving priority to reading as an essential activity; (3) fundamental change of consciousness as a reaction to some books; and (4) permeation of the mind by the vivid recollections of reading.[17] Beginning with this classification, Lewis applied it to the experience of reading in ways that cut across all conventional categories. For instance, he noted that the bad reader, who does not give priority or full attention to reading, will find good writing "either too spare for his purpose or too full. A woodland scene by D. H. Lawrence or a mountain valley by Ruskin gives him far more than he knows what to do with; on the other hand, he would be dissatisfied with Malory's 'he arrived afore a castle which was rich and fair and there was a postern opened towards the sea, and was open without any keeping, save two lions kept the entry and the moon shone clear.'"[18] The bad reader complains about too much description in Hardy or not enough in Hemingway. Lewis assumed that his readers were not in this category, but he feared that their innate responses to literature might be stifled by the critics, the scholars, the experts—in other words, by the classifiers. His inclusion in one passage of D. H. Lawrence, Ruskin, and Malory as examples of good writing cuts across even some of his own criticism. Although Lewis often referred disparagingly to Lawrence as the prime representative of trends he disliked in contemporary literature, he could still appreciate his descriptive powers. The main point was to encourage good readers to ignore classifications, to make their own judgments.

The most obvious example of Lewis's use of classification as a deliberate pedagogical technique is in *English Literature in the Sixteenth Century*. The epithets "Drab" and "Golden" for two periods of the century (as discussed above in Chapter IV) function as labels for two categories of literature. Lewis's insistence that these terms are descriptive, not evaluative, cannot be taken at face value; the connotations of poverty and wealth are too obvious to be ignored, though Lewis gives a different focus in his definition of "Golden" as "not simply good poetry, but poetry which is, so to speak, innocent or ingenuous. In a Golden Age the right thing to do is obvious: 'good is as visible as green!' The great age of Greek sculpture was similarly 'golden.'"[19] Although Lewis showed that some Drab poetry was good and much Golden poetry was bad, there is no question about his preference. His purpose, however, was double-edged. The primary theme of the book is repudiation of the conventional classifications of *Renaissance* and *humanist*. The categories "Drab" and "Golden" are proposed as convenient alternatives for distinguishing major features of an arbitrarily designated period, but they serve also to discredit humanism and discount the Renaissance. If those well-entrenched concepts can be replaced by "Drab" and "Golden," the implication is that all categories are suspect, including Lewis's own. Here the "fathomlessly learned" don is engaged in some splendid leg pulling. The student is provoked to challenge every assignment to either category—in other words, to read the works and make his own judgments, which will in turn be open to challenge.

Within the category of Golden poetry, Lewis found bad as well as good writing. The Elizabethan habit of rhyming on unstressed syllables, practiced by the greatest as well as the weakest poets, was both unpleasing and inexplicable to him. He gave it mock attention by inventing a label, "Simpsonian rhyme," "as we name Bright's disease after him who diagnosed it."[20] Further classification analyzed this affliction in an academic parody. Lewis distinguished basic Simpsonian A (as in *cupid* rhymed with *chid*), Simpsonian A_2 (from thee/to me), Simpsonian A_3 (inextricable/importable), and Plusquam-Simpsonian or Simpsonian B (abashed/saluted). All this detailed classification of what Lewis considered a weakness in Golden poetry can be criticized or dismissed as facetiousness. Some scholars are irritated by Lewis's intrusion of scholarly jokes. He frequently implied that his colleagues took themselves and their critical endeavors too seriously; but his main concern was that the student should not limit himself to pedantic classifications which can be substitutes for understanding and appreciation.

In calling attention to a minor sixteenth-century poet whose work illustrates perfectly the transition from Drab to Golden, Lewis summed up the difference between his early and his late work with a simple metaphor: "Breton has exchanged his boots for pumps."[21] The next sentence, beginning a new paragraph, generalizes his significance: "Breton, then, is such a poet as the historian (not the general reader) sighs for: a textbook case, a human thermometer."[22] Here Lewis, writing a literary history, included himself among the scholars not to be taken too seriously. In his preceding metaphor, the obvious contrast between the field and the court, between clumping and dancing, reinforces the distinction already established between the Drab and the Golden. The change, however, seems superficial: the choice of footwear depends on circumstances and fashion; thus, the metaphor operates at a second level to limit Breton's significance and prepare for his dismissal as a "textbook case." The textbook cases are, of course, necessary. Lewis's classification of sixteenth-century poetry, though often undermined by his own sense of humor, provided a structure within which all the writers could be conveniently accommodated. There are clear indications in every chapter of the teacher's approach to the material. Immediately after the joking reference to Breton as a textbook case, Lewis gave three characteristics of the Golden lyric, as precisely differentiated as in a textbook or in good lecture notes.[23]

The specifically pedagogic techniques used in everything Lewis wrote about literature are notable features of a style that sets him apart from many of his fellow critics and scholars. Whether he was addressing students or a more general audience, Lewis was often provocative, sometimes even belligerent. As he led from the familiar to the unfamiliar, he often revealed the familiar in an unexpected light. As he classified material in unexpected ways, he defied conventional classifications. He constantly incited his readers to think points through from different perspectives. Not only in his arguments but in the style itself Lewis was a challenger.

An individual style is such a closely woven texture that it is sometimes difficult to distinguish warp from woof, to recognize particular strands. For purposes of illustration, I have identified three features of Lewis's style that are characteristic of his writing about literature (in his specifically religious works there are notable similarities).

Following Lewis's own habit of classification, I call these features Mixed Metaphor, Incongruous Imagery, and Artificial Analogy. If these labels sound like subheadings for a warning chapter in a composition text, they fulfil my intention. Lewis took liberties that would be dangerous for a less skillful writer; he was willing to take risks in order to startle the reader out of mental lethargy and to bring the imagination as well as the reason into play.

One of the most striking examples of Lewis's Mixed Metaphors comes from his original conclusion to an after-dinner speech to the members of the Edinburgh Sir Walter Scott Club. In the published text there is no metaphoric language; the simplicity of style appeals directly to the audience:

> You may feel that I have spent too much time on this great author's faults and too little on his excellences. But that is because I am speaking among friends. Where else does one mention the faults of a man one loves? And Scott today has few friends. Our juniors are ill at ease in his presence.[24]

Lewis's typescript in the society's files shows a different version of this passage. I hope this is the way he read it:

> . . . Where else does one mention the faults of a man one loves? Put me to fight for him among his detractors and I'll see the dogs starved before I fling the smallest concession to them. I should not have far to seek for such an audience. In thirty years experience as a tutor I have made one convert, one only, to Scott, and I have met only two or three who loved him already. His stock is far down at present.[25]

This statement, marked for deletion in Lewis's handwriting, is in striking contrast to the printed text. It expresses Lewis's fierce partisanship with a metaphor in which Scott's detractors are metamorphosed from warriors to dogs and then restored to human form as an audience; the juxtaposition is almost as startling as Hamlet's "take arms against a sea of troubles." Here at the end of the address, the dog metaphor reappears to link with a story told in the introduction about Scott and a dog. Thus the mixed metaphor is not a weakness but a strength, not careless but calculated. Why, then, did he change his mind about it? Presumably the emotion as well as the admission was to be shared only among friends.

Lewis's mixed metaphors always had a mixed purpose. His comment on the style of Hooker's sixteenth-century prose is typical: ". . . very few of Hooker's beauties can be picked like flowers and taken home: you must enjoy them where they grow—as you enjoy a twenty-acre field of ripe wheat. Always an artist, he is never merely an artist. He does not reject eloquence, but he has broken and bitted her and taught her the manage. She is perfectly subdued to his task; her high mettle shows through her obedience."[26] The image of the highly bred horse is not offered as an alternative to the metaphors of flowers and fields; there is an illogical shift from the concept of stylistic features as organic to the concept of the stylist as a trainer. But the inconsistent metaphors are linked by a higher consistency: the concept of discipline. It takes a second glance or second thought to realize that the metaphor is indeed mixed, and a third to discover that the mixture makes deeper sense.

Lewis sometimes used individual metaphors in a mixed series, thus offering a variety of alternative ways of illustrating a difficult point. He recognized the difficulty modern readers might have in understanding the concept of discipline implicit in Milton:

For this is perhaps the central paradox of his vision. Discipline, while the world is yet unfallen, exists for the sake of what seems its very opposite—for freedom, almost for extravagance. The pattern deep hidden in the dance, hidden so deep that shallow spectators cannot see it, alone gives beauty to the wild, free gestures that fill it, just as the decasyllabic norm gives beauty to all the licences and variations of the poet's verse. The happy soul is, like a planet, a *wandering* star; yet in that very wandering (as astronomy teaches) invariable; she is eccentric beyond all predicting, yet equable in her eccentricity. The heavenly frolic arises from an orchestra which is in tune; the rules of courtesy make perfect ease and freedom possible between those who obey them. Without sin, the universe is a solemn Game: and there is no good game without rules.[27]

Here there are two illustrations (the dance and the rules of courtesy) and three metaphors (the planet, the orchestra, the game). Since a paradox cannot be explained logically, this choice of metaphors appeals to the imagination instead. All three are harmonious in tone, representing the unity of diverse elements that is their common factor.

Another example in which the mixture of metaphor stresses the point is a passage describing the tone of Augustine's *Confessions*: "He is lost and bewildered. Every new path in this country excites his curiosity and his awe. Why did he rob the pear tree? Why does tragedy please? He worries such problems as a dog worries a bone. He wanders hither and thither in his own mind and speaks the language of a traveller."[28] Here the paragraph, like its subject, reveals a subtle bewilderment. The juxtaposition of the saint's soul-searching and the dog's antics is a surprise. The image of the traveler comes back to the point from a different angle, as the searcher goes round in circles. The traveler is a conventional image in this context, the dog an unusual one. The reader must remain on the alert, never knowing what to expect next.

Many of Lewis's mixed metaphors also qualify for the category of Incongruous Imagery, the intrusion of an incongruous image in a passage otherwise serious and not satirical. In its simplest form, the incongruity occurs as an example rather than as figurative language. Lewis justified the concept of obedience in Milton as "the commonest of themes; even Peter Rabbit came to grief because he *would* go into Mr. McGregor's garden."[29] The surprise here includes the implication that Milton need not be so difficult to understand as modern readers expect. This use of the homely style in a literary context goes beyond the teacher's purpose of relating to what the student is familiar with; the incongruity is so striking that it must be significant per se.

Incongruity is most conspicuous in *English Literature in the Sixteenth-Century.* The volume's position in the Oxford History of English Literature series, the wide-ranging erudition of its author, and the sheer weight of its 685 pages all lead the reader to expect high seriousness; he is not prepared for Lewis to explain the artistic failure of an early Spenser poem by saying ". . . that Spenser's ample Muse was unwise ever to appear in public without the *corsage* of stanzaic form."[30] Another image relating style to dress explains the lack of artistry in a minor Elizabethan prose writer: ". . . the rhetoric of such an author is laid on as an extra. Munday did not dream of being 'literary' when he had in hand work which would be bought only for its matter. He wears his 'dicky' only when waiting at table."[31] These humorous images might at first glance seem to ridicule both writers thus characterized. However, the distinction between them is greater than the similarity: Spenser is associated with divine inspiration, Munday with menial service. Even the beloved Spenser may be teased at times, but Munday must be recognized as engaged in commerce rather than in literature.

The incongruity of a commercial image may function much more subtly. Lewis deplored the trend, beginning as early as the sixteenth century, for writers to follow their own creative impulses regardless of public taste or demand: "It may well be that the author who claims to write neither for patron nor public but for himself has done our art incalculable harm and bred up infinite charlatans by teaching us to emphasize the public's duty of 'recognition' instead of the artist's duty to teach and delight. Things may have been better when you could order your ode from Pindar as you ordered your wine from the wine merchant."[32] The shock effect here might seem at first to ridicule the idea of poetry produced to supply demand, but the full force of the image reverses that impression. The equation of poetry with wine sets up subliminal echoes of such familiar passages as "beakerful of the warm South" or "Burst Joy's grape against his palate fine," yet none of the immemorial symbolism associated with wine can obscure the simple fact that the way to be sure of getting the best quality is to order from an expert. The emphasis is on the relationship between the artist and the public in an ordered society. Lewis ridiculed the thought of the artist creating for himself rather than for his public in another incongruous image describing John Donne: he said that the metaphysical love poet wrote "like an oyster turning his disease into a pearl."[33] The result is indeed a pearl, perhaps of great price, but the reader must prise open a shell to get it. The reminder of the oyster's disease indicates Lewis's disagreement with many critics about the position and value of Donne.

Lewis used incongruous images particularly to disparage the contemporary critical attitudes and theories that he distrusted. Referring to a contemporary of Spenser who recognized potential power in *The Shepherd's Calendar,* Lewis said this critic revealed no particular discrimination because "to hear young men proclaiming that their circle or someone whom their circle has 'taken up' is the only hope for poetry is no more wonder than to see a goose go barefoot."[34] Here the link between fashionable critics and geese is merely by association. In a more detailed image, Lewis pointed out the mistake of a particular group of critics in terms so incongruous that analysis is submerged in ridicule. The Elizabethan sonnet sequences, he said, are often disparaged by critics who do not know how to read them. "Critics reading them, as they were never meant to be read, hastily and in bulk, are gorged and satiated with beauty, as a fish can be choked by holding its head upstream. The water is good water but there is too much of it for the fish."[35] This is typical of an incongruous metaphor to which Lewis gave an extra twist: such critics are not fish out of water, but creatures disoriented in their own habitat.

Such incongruous imagery makes it clear why those who agree with Lewis enjoy reading his scholarly and critical works, while those who disagree are often antagonized. Fish, geese, oysters, dogs, and dinosaurs, even Peter Rabbit, and innumerable inanimate objects equally out of place in serious literary discussion keep popping up as unexpectedly as anything in *Alice in Wonderland.* They are startling in contrast to other passages with powerfully congruent imagery. In an analysis of the effects of rhetoric, Lewis linked three images whose connotations reinforce and even demonstrate the thesis:

> ... Mr. Eliot speaks of "music heard so deeply that it is not heard at all." Only as we emerge from the mode of consciousness induced by the symphony do we begin once more to attend explicitly to the sounds which induced it. In the same way, when we are caught up into the experience which a "grand" style communicates, we are, in a sense, no longer conscious of the style. Incense is consumed by being used. The poem kindles admirations which leave us no leisure to admire the poem. When our participation in a rite becomes perfect we think no more of ritual, but are engrossed by that *about which* the rite is performed; but afterwards we recognize that the ritual was the sole method by which this concentration could be achieved.[36]

When Lewis's imagery is harmonious, as in this passage, the reader is not particularly aware of stylistic techniques. When he used mixed metaphors and incongruent imagery, he startled the reader and caused him to sharpen and redirect his attention. The most startling of his techniques is the Artificial Analogy.

The distinction between metaphor and analogy is not clear-cut. In the passage quoted above, the images of the symphony, the incense, and the ritual are used for connotative and illustrative purposes; no real argument is involved. But it is only a short step from such imagery to the analogy used as the basis for an argument. Somewhere on this limited continuum is the analogy in Lewis's argument about poetic fashion in the sixteenth century: "After Tottel the greatest composite monument of the Drab Age is the *Mirror for Magistrates*. In a way, just because it is so much worse, it reveals the movement of taste more clearly than Tottel—as a derelict shows the set of the tide more clearly than a ship under sail."[37] This vivid picture, which makes the point effectively, disintegrates in the light of logic. If books can be imagined as ships in a sea of public taste, then the book most indicative of that taste cannot be a derelict. The difference between derelict and "ship under sail" is fundamental, not just "so much worse." The comparison is so far-fetched that it will not bear the weight of argument. This is an example of analogy that is artificial rather than false: the result of artifice rather than of nature, deliberately contrived but not intended to deceive. The argument is offered almost playfully, to challenge rather than to force acceptance of the idea.

A highly developed example of the artificial analogy is used to refute what Lewis called the "modern" idea that only poets can criticize poetry:

> ... we must beware of false parallels. ... As regards a *skill*, such as medicine or engineering, we must distinguish. Only the skilled can judge the skilfulness, but that is not the same as judging the value of the result. It is for cooks to say whether a given dish proves skill in the cook; but whether the product on which this skill has been lavished is worth eating or no is a question on which a cook's opinion is of no particular value. We may *therefore* [italics mine] allow poets to tell us (at least if they are experienced in the same *kind* of composition) whether it is easy or difficult to write like Milton, but not whether the reading of Milton is a valuable experience. For who can endure a doctrine which would allow only dentists to say whether our teeth were aching, only cobblers to say whether our shoes hurt us, and only governments to tell us whether we were being well governed?[38]

The word *therefore* makes this a full-fledged argument from analogy, but the introductory warning against the false parallels set up by others alerts the reader to the deliberate artificiality of Lewis's own parallels.

Such arguments from analogy are particularly characteristic of *A Preface to Paradise Lost,* where Lewis was implicitly defending Milton against his modern detractors. Although the word *therefore* does not appear in this passage about Milton's use of the epic form, the analogies are clearly argumentative.

> The parallel is not to be found in a modern author considering what his unique message is and what idiom will best convey it, but rather in a gardener asking whether he will make a rockery *or* a tennis court, an architect asking whether he is to make a church *or* a house, a boy debating whether to play hockey *or* football, a man hesitating between marriage and celibacy. The things between which choice is to be made already exist in their own right, each with a character of its own well established in the public world and governed by its own laws. If you choose one, you lose the specific beauties and delights of the other; for your aim is not mere excellence, but the excellence proper to the thing chosen—the goodness of a rockery or a celibate being different from that of a tennis court or a husband.[39]

Here the incongruous juxtapositions in the last sentence call attention to the fact that the parallels may be artificial as far as argument is concerned.

Lewis's artificial analogies are so blatant that they cannot be explained as conscious or unconscious logical fallacies. Instead, Lewis was deliberately challenging the authority of logic by exaggerating its methods, in order to appeal not to the reason but to the imagination. For instance, in defending Milton against the charge of heresy, Lewis said the only suggestion of the doctrine of latent evil in God was a passage in *Paradise Lost* (V,

117-119) where Adam tells Eve that evil can enter the mind of God or Man without approval and hence without evil effects. Lewis then argued: "Since the whole point of Adam's remark is that the approval of the will alone makes a mind evil and that the presence of evil as an object of thought does not—and since our own common sense tells us that we no more become bad by thinking of badness than we become triangular by thinking of triangles—this passage is wholly inadequate to support the astonishing doctrine attributed to Milton."[40] The whimsical analogy here referred to "our common sense," totally ignoring the noncomparable components of badness and triangles, takes the point beyond the limits of logic.

Trained as he was in the discipline of logic, first by the stern tutor who prepared him for Oxford and later by the study of philosophy in the Greats curriculum at Oxford, renowned though he was as a formidable dialectician, Lewis as a stylist is easily identified by his strikingly artificial analogies. Typical of the argument based on farfetched comparison, developed with sweeping generalization and oversimplification, is the conclusion of *A Preface to Paradise Lost*. Explaining why different categories of readers no longer enjoy Milton, Lewis analyzed various critical approaches; he argued that those who consider Milton's artistic selectivity unrealistic are deluded by admirers of the stream-of-consciousness technique:

> The disorganized consciousness which it regards as specially real is in fact highly artificial. It is discovered by introspection—that is, by artificially suspending all the normal and outgoing activities of the mind and then attending to what is left. . . . The poet who finds by introspection that the soul is mere chaos is like a police-

man who, having himself stopped all the traffic in a certain street, should then solemnly write down in his notebook "The stillness in this street is highly suspicious." It can very easily be shown that the unselective chaos of images and momentary desires which introspection discovers is not the essential characteristic of consciousness. For consciousness is, from the outset, selective, and ceases when selection ceases. . . . When the voice of your friend or the page of your book sinks into democratic equality with the pattern of the wallpaper, the feel of your clothes, your memory of last night, and the noises from the road, you are falling asleep.[41]

Here the analogies from ordinary life reinforce through their realism the concept of selectivity as more *realistic* than stream of consciousness. As the burden of proof shifts to the other side, rebuttal is of course equally easy. To create an artistic impression of the stream of consciousness requires conscious control; Joyce and Woolf were as selective as Milton. Lewis's focus was not on modern writers but on critics who evaluate a seventeenth-century writer by criteria of the twentieth.

The final point in Lewis's *apologia* for Milton concerns not misunderstanding of the style of epic poetry but disapproval of its implications:

If Mr. Eliot disdains the eagles and trumpets of epic poetry because the fashion of this world passes away, I honour him. But if he goes on to draw the conclusion that all poetry should have the penitential qualities of his own best work, I believe he is mistaken. As long as we live in merry middle earth, it is necessary to have middle things. If the round table is abolished, for every one who rises to the level of Galahad, a hundred will drop plumb down to that of Mordred. Mr. Eliot may succeed in persuading the reading youth of England to have done with robes of purple and pavements of marble. But he will not therefore find them walking in sackcloth on floors of mud—he will only find them in smart, ugly suits walking on rubberoid. It has all been tried before. The older Puritans took away the maypoles and the mincepies: but they did not bring in the millennium, they only brought in the Restoration. Galahad must not make common cause with Mordred, for it is always Mordred who gains, and he who loses, by such alliance.[42]

Followers of Lewis will hear echoes in this passage of some of his familiar themes subtly interwoven. He was concerned with "the reading youth of England," those for whom he felt directly or indirectly the teacher's responsibility. He deplored any teaching that persuaded the young that the grandeur of old literature was artificial and unrelated to their lives. The analogy of the Round Table is the central point in the defense of Milton's epic: here Lewis emphasized not the spiritual but the heroic implications of the Arthurian myth. The associated images of "eagles and trumpets," of "robes of purple and pavements of marble," are both classical and Biblical. The alternative to the hero, he suggested, is not the saint but the nonentity—or the traitor. Rejecting both alternatives, we must at least reconsider before rejecting Milton.

In this coda to *A Preface to Paradise Lost,* Lewis seemed to be appealing particularly to his fellow teachers. Many faculty members as well as students were in the audience for the series of university lectures from which the book was developed. Although the stated purpose of the last section was to refute the arguments of various detractors of Milton, the analogy used in the final paragraph placed the whole subject in a broader context. An underlying implication is that the teacher who would want to be a Galahad is in danger of making common cause with Mordred.

In his writing, as in his teaching, Lewis spoke to colleagues, to students, to all the company of those who love reading and recognize its contribution to the good life. More knowledgeable and more experienced than many readers, Lewis guided the extension and expansion of their reading experience. He believed that knowledge imparted could be useful—but only as basic equipment, as a set of tools. The ability to use the tools and to create something meaningful with them must be nurtured. This was what Lewis constantly did in all of his writing about literature; while imparting information about the wide range of literature that he knew intimately, he always intended to raise rather than to settle questions, to arouse rather than to satisfy curiosity. His provocative style was a counterpoint to his erudite matter. By challenging other authorities, he forced the reader to think for himself. By delighting or startling the reader with unexpected links between the familiar and the unfamiliar, Lewis encouraged him to respond imaginatively. Even the professor's leg-pulling incongruities of style had their purpose of preventing his students and all his readers from taking either Lewis or themselves too seriously.

Chapter VII

THE PROPHETIC THEME

*Without a parable modern physics speaks
not to the multitudes.* —THE DISCARDED
IMAGE

Lewis himself provided the model opening paragraph
for the final chapter of a book about literature or a
literary figure. In his study of Charles Williams's
Arthurian poetry, he began the conclusion with characteristic reservations:

> So far I have been trying to explain rather than to
> judge. In this last chapter I shall put forward a few
> guesses as to the permanent place of this poem in English
> literature. More than guesses they cannot be. The history
> of a poem is only beginning when it is first printed. We
> cannot be sure that posterity will be any wiser than we,
> but they are not likely to be foolish in exactly the same
> ways. A work of art has to be seen in many different lights
> and to test itself against many different kinds of capacity
> and experience before it finds its level.[1]

The suggestion that posterity may or may not be wiser
than we, that their judgments are bound to be different,
is an example of Lewis's attempt to overcome the "chronological snobbery" of those who judge the past from the
point of view of the present as if that were an absolute.

Sometimes Lewis seemed to be guilty of chronological snobbery in reverse, that is, of assuming that the past was superior to the present. His designation of himself as "Old Western Man" can be thus interpreted, his role seen as exemplary—but Lewis's emphasis was on the exemplar as illustration or specimen, not as model for imitation. The dinosaur image does not idealize the past. Lewis's frequent disparagement of the present "period" was a deliberate corrective to some moderns' patronizing attitudes toward earlier periods, as in his back-handed compliment to the humanists for overcoming the medieval idea that a gentleman should not be a scholar: "The tradition of gentlemanly philistinism slowly but surely decayed and was not reinstated till compulsory games altered the whole character of school life. There was thus a long lucid interval between Squire Western and Bertie Wooster; it is arguable that during that interval England was at her greatest."[2] (The interjection of such a comment by a bookworm who had detested team sports at boarding school is typical of the flavor of personal bias in Lewis's criticism: the point is tangential to the context, the argument facetious.) But Lewis's attack on philistinism was incidental to the underlying theme of incalculable fluctuations in history. If the lucid interval began after Fielding's Squire Western, it took more than two hundred years for the humanists' ideas of education to triumph; in less than two hundred years philistinism was resurgent in Wodehouse's Bertie. What Lewis intimated here, as an aside, is the tentative nature of all historical judgments.

Lewis's warning about chronological snobbery was echoed by the historian C. V. Wedgwood in the 1957 Leslie Stephen lecture at Cambridge. Acknowledging the debt of historical scholarship to the romantic and imaginative approach to history, she warned against "the smugness which treated the past chiefly as something which could be compared to its disadvantage with the present, so as to demonstrate gratifying human progress."[3] Her emphasis on the way we invest the past with our present habits of thought must have been approved by Lewis (if he was in the audience) and recognized by his students as the obstacle to understanding of literature that he tried to remove in his criticism.

The difficulty of evaluating one period from the perspective of another made Lewis wary of predictions. In his uncertainty about the continuing reputation of Spenser, Lewis sounded an elegiac note, deploring the loss of the "ordered exuberance of the *Faerie Queene*."[4] In this and other parts of *English Literature in the Sixteenth Century,* Lewis gave the impression of nostalgia for the past, disapproval of the present, and pessimism about the future. Some of his specific reasons for this attitude were suggested in a passage written nearly twenty years earlier, when he had made a more confident prediction about Spenser. He expected that the "romantic conception of marriage," on which the *Faerie Queene* was based, would become interesting as an outmoded curiosity:

> The whole conception is now being attacked. Feminism in politics, reviving ascetism in religion, animalism in imaginative literature, and, above all, the discoveries of the psychoanalysts, have undermined that monogamic idealism about sex which served us for three centuries. Whether society will gain or lose by the revolution, I need not try to predict; but Spenser ought to gain. What once was a platitude should now have for some the brave appeal of a cause nearly lost, and for others the interest of a highly specialized historical phenomenon—the peculiar flower of a peculiar civilization, important whether for good or ill and well worth our understanding.[5]

Lewis's sympathies were clearly with that "peculiar civilization." There are, however, other facets of his view to be considered. Another of his judgments of Spenser applies to Lewis himself: "He was often sad: but not, at bottom, worried. To many of my readers such a state of mind must appear a total illusion. If they cannot suspend their disbelief, they should leave Spenser alone; there are plenty of other authors to read. They must not, however, suppose that he was under an illusion about the historical world. That is not where he differs from them. He differs from them in thinking that it is not the whole story."[6] For Lewis, as for Spenser, both past and present are chapters in the whole story, *sub specie aeternitas.*

As a critic, Lewis had set out to promote Owen Barfield's theory of history, neither venerating nor patronizing the past and recognizing the present as merely another period. This aim was given additional impetus by the influence of Charles Williams, whose novels Lewis had admired before they became friends when Williams moved from London to Oxford during World War II. Williams's interest in the Arthurian heritage as the native imaginative tradition of England was not limited to its significance in literature: he believed that the Grail story is still operative in history, that the forces of evil in the real world of the twentieth century must be overcome by Christian champions. Williams revealed this conflict in fictional settings that "mix what some people call the realistic and the fantastic. . . . We meet in them, on the one hand, very ordinary modern people who talk the slang of our own day, and live in the suburbs: on the other hand, we also meet the supernatural—ghosts, magicians, and archetypal beasts."[7] Although Williams was a sophisticated intellectual writing on a different plane from those who concentrate on the number 666 as the sign of the beast or identify Satanism in familiar commercial symbols, he was equally certain that the evidence of supernatural conflict is apparent in our daily environment.

Lewis evoked the Arthurian tradition as metaphor in the finale of *A Preface to Paradise Lost*; writing during the war that threatened Britain and Western civilization, he reminded his contemporaries of threats from within. The purpose of the book was to identify and dispel misunderstandings that prevented full appreciation of *Paradise Lost*. These relate not only to the nature of the epic but also to the nature of good and evil: Galahad and Mordred. In this context Lewis's Arthurian allusion would not be associated with Williams if the book were not dedicated to him. Lewis defended *Paradise Lost* in terms of the heroic tradition. Of those who now reject this heritage he said, "It has all been tried before." His reference to "the maypoles and the mincepies" taken away by the Puritans seems unrelated to the Round Table, but with Lewis there is usually a deliberate link in the most apparently disparate imagery. He had illustrated "ordered exuberance" in epic poetry with metaphors of dancing and feasting. Those ceremonies associated with the court were shared by the commoners on traditional occasions like May Day and Christmas: pagan and Christian elements fuse in the observance of these festivals, as they do in the Arthurian myth. The Puritans tried, without success, to stamp out the native tradition, and got something worse. Lewis implied that what has been tried before may well be tried again, and the results may well be very different from the intentions. Perennial forces will continue to operate in unexpected ways, as they do in all of Charles Williams's novels and in *That Hideous Strength,* Lewis's experiment in the Williams mode, which he called a "fairy-tale for grown-ups."

Although Charles Williams has had a small following of devoted readers and some serious critical attention, it is doubtless his connection with C. S. Lewis that has led to recent American paperback editions of his novels (first published in the 1930s). In each story, ordinary urban or provincial twentieth-century England is invaded, not by creatures from outer space but by omnipresent forces. A dead woman revisits a friend, figures from the Tarot pack come to life, an archaeologist and a stockbroker control an ancient Persian relic of great power, a girl experiences physically the suffering of an ancestor executed in the seventeenth century—these are a characteristic sample of supernatural events in completely realistic settings, part of the daily experience of believers or nonbelievers. The form of each plot is that of a thriller; the issue is a soul's salvation or damnation.

In addition to seven novels, works of theology and criticism, and several plays, Williams left unfinished at his sudden death in 1945 a prose study of the figure of Arthur and a cycle of lyrical poems about Arthur, his court poet Taliessin, and various knights of the Round Table. Thirty-two of the poems had been published by the Oxford University Press in two volumes, *Taliessin Through Logres* and *The Region of the Summer Stars*, but the cycle was incomplete. Lewis had discussed the poems with Williams and wanted to help readers come to terms with their allusive difficulties by rearranging them in their imaginary chronological order. "Sometimes I am in doubt; and I hope that the fame of the poem will not grow so slowly but that before I die I may see 'Williams scholarship' sweeping my whole chronology away and allotting me my place among the pre-scientific primitives."[8] The hope for the poem, the gentle mockery of "scholarship," and the genuine recognition that his own views might be superseded are all characteristic. Throughout the hundred pages of lucid and detailed commentary, Lewis frequently mentioned his uncertainty about individual images, allusions, even syntax. Lewis as teacher guided the reader without claiming to know all the answers. His hope for the fame of the poem was not realized in his lifetime, nor in the next two decades. "Williams scholarship" has concentrated on the novels, and the main interest in Williams has been his association with Lewis and Tolkien in the Inklings group; it is still too soon to judge whether Williams's visionary world of Camelot and Taliessin's unicorn will appeal to the imagination of another generation as they did to Lewis.

The influence of Charles Williams is evident throughout *That Hideous Strength*: in the realistic contemporary setting, the carefully drawn emotional and spiritual conflicts of an intellectual young husband and wife, the physical immanence of supernatural forces, the domesticated bear and the severed head, the prophetic dreams. All these features give Lewis's third novel a form so different from the first two that the term "trilogy" seems a misnomer—yet they are related thematically through the recurrent supernatural powers revealed to the space traveler in the first two books. This character is no longer a protagonist because for him the *agony* was accomplished in *Perelandra*. The man who was Arthur Ransom, the philologist, has become the Pendragon, the secret Arthur in the unbroken succession of heirs to the tradition that Williams celebrated in his Arthurian poems. He and his small band of followers are prepared for the intervention of Merlin that resolves the conflict of this plot. The novel ends with a temporary victory of good over evil.

The Arthurian theme touches an imaginative chord perhaps more responsive in the United States today than in England. The appeal of the Kennedy administration in the early 1960s was defined by explicit reference to Camelot, and one implicit element in the 1980 presidential speculation was whether the sole surviving Kennedy represents Galahad or Mordred. College students reading *That Hideous Strength* in a seminar on Lewis enjoy discussing who will become the next Pendragon in the novel and in current history. The youth of this country have been searching for causes to fight for—and against. They have been fascinated by *The Lord of the Rings,* by *Star Trek* and *Star Wars.* The heroic tradition still appeals.

The imaginative power generated by Lewis's interpretation of Williams's Arthurian poetry inspired one Oxford undergraduate to express his appreciation in a form that must have delighted Lewis:

Logres

To C.W. and C.S.L.

A young knight in the Waste Land of his heart
  Who turned from Saxon pillage, yet scarce knew
  What Rome had left, save in its outward view
Of code and rule, of castle, town and mart,—
Sought for the Grail in faery lands apart
  And found it not until he met with Two,
  God's bard and prophet, and their teaching drew
His feet to where the realms of Arthur start.
Taliessin passed, as one of too much worth,
  Into the region of the summer stars,
Leaving his voice behind. But *Merlin* here
Still teaches us to see how bright and clear
  The realm of Arthur lives, unstained of wars,
Logres, until the Kingdom come on Earth.[9]

The student was Roger Lancelyn Green, who became Lewis's lifelong friend and one of his biographers. To Green, Lewis dedicated his last book, *The Discarded Image,* which epitomizes his central message about the powers and limits of the imagination.

In this book, Green's "prophet" proclaimed the same message that he had introduced in his first: Barfield's theory and practice regarding the past and the present.

Again his explanation of a medieval concept was designed first of all to enable readers to understand the literature. The medieval Model of the Universe is now a "discarded image" because it no longer satisfies the conditions of our experience. We cannot understand the medieval author's intentions unless we can visualize the Model from which he worked; but Lewis's fundamental intention in reconstructing this Model was to "induce us to regard all Models in the right way, respecting each and idolizing none. . . . No Model is a catalogue of ultimate realities, and none is a mere fantasy."[10] Here is the core of all Lewis's teaching. The models of the past have been "discarded" as no longer valid, but we need not give them up; we can still respect and enjoy past models, recognizing that our own models, in turn, will be superseded. In any period, Lewis said, "The great masters do not take any Model quite so seriously as the rest of us. They know that it is, after all, only a model, possibly replaceable."[11]

Lewis was a great enough master to avoid taking any model too seriously. He observed in a letter to Barfield that the scientific model of animal behavior was inconsistent with experience: "Talking of beasts and birds, have you ever noticed this contrast: that when you read a scientific account of any animal's life you get an impression of laborious, incessant, almost rational economic activity, . . . but when you study any animal you know, what at once strikes you is their cheerful fatuity, the pointlessness of nearly all they do. Say what you like, Barfield, the world is sillier and better fun than they make out."[12] Here he was whimsical. In other contexts he speculated with a light touch but absolute seriousness about the possibility that our models will be replaced: "One often wonders how different the content of our faith will look when we see it in the total context. Might it be as if one were living in an infinite earth? Further knowledge wd. leave our map of the Atlantic say, quite *correct,* but if it turned out to be the estuary of a great river—and the continent through which that river flowed turned out to be itself an island—off the shores of a still greater continent—and so on. You see what I mean? Not one jot of Revelation will be proved false; but so many new truths might be added."[13]

Lewis's idea of replacing models usually implied adding rather than discarding: since "none is a mere fantasy," all may have some value. His concept of models was closely related to his ideas about myth. Trying to convince a correspondent that *The Fellowship of the Ring* was not an allegory, Lewis first recommended Tolkien's explanation of his views, "On Fairy-Stories," in *Essays Presented to Charles Williams.* Then Lewis gave his own: "*My* view wd. be that a good myth (i.e. a story out of which ever varying meanings will grow for different readers and in different ages) is a higher thing than an allegory (into which *one* meaning has been put). Into an allegory a man can put only what he already knows; in a myth he puts what he does not yet know and cd. not come by in any other way."[14] Lewis was always aware of how much man "does not know yet."

The realization that our models are not sacrosanct, that our myths are parts of a greater story, pervades Lewis's fiction. His children's stories included talking beasts, a concept from the preliterary human imagination. Swift's rational horses, the Houyhnhnms, and their anthropoid savage beasts, the Yahoos, were a more complex development of this tradition, which has continued in *Animal Farm* and *Watership Down* as well as in children's fiction. For Lewis, however, the talking beasts and other nonhuman characters are more than literary convention. In the first Narnian chronicle, another dimension is suggested during the little girl's first encounter with a faun. While Mr. Tumnus is laying the table for tea, Lucy looks at the books on his shelves: "They had titles like *The Life and Loves of Silenus* or *Nymphs and Their Ways* or *Men, Monks and Gamekeepers: a Study in Popular Legend* or *Is Man a Myth?*"[15] (In the television adaptation of the book, the titles are shown on the screen while Lucy reads them aloud, thus emphasizing the importance that she is unaware of.) Being a child, Lucy is not concerned that the factual in one world may appear as "legend" or "myth" in another.

The first two stories in Lewis's space trilogy are based on his concept of different models for truth in other worlds. In *Out of the Silent Planet,* the human traveler learns that the Malacandrians had no idea that there was intelligent life in his world. Ransom's first encounter with a *hross* (something like a penguin, an otter, a seal, and a stoat), a talking nonhuman creature, was an experience "which completely altered his state of mind." Lewis's description of "the first tingling intercourse of two different, but rational, species," which is climaxed by the offer and acceptance of a shell cup of wine, illustrates memorably the interaction of new models and changeless realities.[16] An even more striking version of this concept is the model of unfallen innocence in *Perelandra,* where Ransom, on the planet that we call Venus, meets a Green Lady whose home is a Floating Island. For her the prohibition essential to the theme is that she may not stay overnight on the Fixed Land. The familiar imagery of firm foundations is not easy to abandon, but the twofold meaning is not ambiguous. In this novel, as in the Narnia stories, Lewis meant that man cannot rely on stability, permanence, or any kind of natural security—his only security is in faith and obedience. But the images are not intended as allegory. Lewis created different worlds with different systems of time and space as well as different models of relationship with the Creator.

Some of Lewis's new imaginative models have been disturbing to those who cannot see their own models as replaceable. In *The Great Divorce*, Lewis pictured Hell as a gray city with free bus service to the bright, cool, mountain landscape of Heaven. Yet there was no "marriage of heaven and hell." Lewis showed in his dream vision that their divorce was made inevitable by human choice between good and evil on earth. In the preface he explained the idea that his model illustrated: "But what, you ask, of earth? Earth, I think, will not be found by anyone to be in the end a very distinct place. I think earth, if chosen instead of Heaven, will turn out to have been, all along, only a region in Hell: and earth, if put second to Heaven, to have been from the beginning a part of Heaven itself."[17] But he added a reminder that it was only a model, true in his opinion but not to be taken literally: "I beg readers to remember that this is a fantasy. It has of course—or I intended it to have—a moral. But the transmortal conditions are solely an imaginative supposal: they are not even a guess or a speculation at what may actually await us. The last thing I wish is to arouse factual curiosity about the details of the after-world."[18] Such curiosity is so basic that it is difficult for some people to distinguish between elements of truth and details of imaginative models.

The same problem sometimes arises with the Narnia stories. Readers recognize the creation of Narnia through the Lion's song as a model based on Genesis.[19] They understand Aslan's self-sacrifice as a model of the Atonement. Yet some of them balk at the acceptance of Emeth, the follower of the false god Tash, into the everlasting Narnia at the climax of *The Last Battle*. His report of his welcome by the Lion makes clear that Aslan and Tash are both *models* of eternal truths:

> " . . . I overcame my fear and questioned the Glorious One and said, Lord, is it then true, as the Ape said, that thou and Tash are one? The Lion growled so that the earth shook (but his wrath was not against me) and said, It is false. Not because he and I are one, but because we are opposites, I take to me the services which thou hast done to him. For I and he are of such different kinds that no service which is vile can be done to me, and none which is not vile can be done to him. . . . unless thy desire had been for me thou wouldst not have sought so long and so truly. For all find what they truly seek."[20]

The truths are absolute but the models are relative, as the immediately succeeding passage makes humorously obvious:

> "And since then, O Kings and Ladies, I have been wandering to find him and my happiness is so great that it even weakens me like a wound. And this is the marvel of marvels, that he called me Beloved, me who am but as a dog—"
>
> "Eh? What's that?" said one of the Dogs.
>
> "Sir," said Emeth. "It is but a fashion of speech which we have in Calormen."
>
> "Well, I can't say it's one I like very much," said the Dog.
>
> "He doesn't mean any harm," said an older Dog. "After all, *we* call our puppies *Boys* when they don't behave properly."
>
> "So we do," said the first Dog. "Or *girls.*"
>
> "S-s-sh!" said the Old Dog. "That's not a nice word to use. Remember where you are."[21]

The joke here reminds us not to take any models too seriously.

Lewis focused consistently on our most precious models as valid but imperfect representations of ultimate realities. The professor from *The Lion, the Witch and the Wardrobe,* now Lord Digory, explains it at the end of *The Last Battle*:

> "Listen Peter. When Aslan said you could never go back to Narnia, he meant the Narnia you were thinking of. But that was not the real Narnia. That had a beginning and an end. It was only a shadow or a copy of the real Narnia which has always been here and always will be here: just as our own world, England and all, is only a shadow or copy of something real in Aslan's real world. You need not mourn over Narnia, Lucy. All of the old Narnia that mattered, all the dear creatures, have been drawn into the real Narnia through the Door. And of course it is different; as different as a real thing is from a shadow or as waking life is from a dream." His voice stirred everyone like a trumpet as he spoke these words: but when he added under his breath "It's all in Plato, all in Plato: bless me, what *do* they teach them at these schools!" the older ones laughed. It was so exactly like the sort of thing they had heard him say long ago in that other world where his beard was grey instead of golden. He knew why they were laughing and joined in the laugh himself.[22]

In the last sentence Lewis was speaking also about his own role, showing that even when he was most serious he did not take himself too seriously.

Throughout his career as critic and teacher, Lewis had concentrated on the imaginative power of the image, the myth, all the various models of absolute reality. Although scholarly emphasis on mythopoeia was avant-garde in the 1950s, Lewis identified it with an intellectual tradition going back at least as far as Plato. As a teacher, he deplored the threatened loss of this tradition. He had to deal with college students unfamiliar with Plato's myth of the cave and image of the divided line: those seminal models for the concept that whatever we can perceive through our senses is merely an approximation of what really is. Through this basic premise of Platonism, the author of the gospel of John explained the Hebrew theme of the Messiah to Gentiles and Jews of Hellenistic background. The counterpart of the Old Testament "In the beginning God . . . " is the New Testament "In the beginning was the Word" (the *Logos,* or the *Idea,* as Plato is sometimes translated). Only once has the Word been made flesh and dwelt among us, in our human history. But our literature has always embodied, in words, the copies or shadows of the Word. No theme was more central to Lewis, yet he recognized that the teaching of Plato is urgent only in the temporal perspective of the gray beard, not in the eternal perspective of the golden.

In his *Christian Herald* article speculating about the possibility of finding rational life on other planets, Lewis emphasized the limitations of our human perspective. He reaffirmed that our history may be only one part of the true story, that our model of sin and salvation may be valid only for our own circumstances. Explicitly he warned that our systematic models must not be imposed where they do not apply; implicitly he suggested that our fantasy models may be facts in other systems. The description of the divine Spirits of Mars and Venus as they appear to Ransom at the end of *Perelandra* illustrates both aspects of this basic concept:

> Their bodies . . . were white. But a flush of diverse colours began at about the shoulders and streamed up

the necks and flickered over face and head and stood out around the head like plumage or a halo. . . . Nothing less like the "angel" of popular art could well be imagined. The rich variety, the hint of undeveloped possibilities, which make the interest of human faces, were entirely absent. One single, changeless expression . . . was stamped on each and there was nothing else there at all. . . . Pure, spiritual, intellectual love shot from their faces like barbed lightning. It was so unlike the love we experience that its expression could easily be mistaken for ferocity. . . . Both the bodies were naked, and both were free from any sexual characteristics, either primary or secondary. . . . Malacandra was like rhythm and Perelandra like melody. . . . Malacandra affected him like a quantitative, Perelandra like an accentual, metre.[23]

Visual features of this model are like the extraterrestrial creatures who communicate with humans by means of music and emerge from their spaceship at the end of *Close Encounters of the Third Kind.*

Certain films in recent years have introduced some of Lewis's interests to an audience even larger than that reached by his books. Tolkien's *The Hobbit* and Lewis's *The Lion, the Witch and the Wardrobe* have been popular in animated versions. The cinema public has been at least exposed to the Arthurian story in *Excalibur,* though the treatment of the material was not consistent. It is intriguing to speculate about whether Lewis would have enjoyed the 1960s film of *King Solomon's Mines* more than he did a 1930s version,[24] and how he would evaluate the different kinds of space fiction and adventure fantasy films of the 1970s and 1980s. He wrote to his close friend Arthur Greeves in 1933: "I was persuaded into going to *King Kong* because it sounded the sort of Rider Haggardish thing that has always exercised a spell over me."[25] Whether the spell worked or not he did not say, but his brother Warren's diary for the same day affirms: "This was as good a film as I have ever seen."[26] When the brothers disagreed, Warren usually included the argument in his diary. Only two other films did he mention their seeing together. One evening during a 1939 walking tour they saw *Snow White*, which, "a few touches of abominable vulgarity apart, is first rate; especially all the scenes in which the animals figure."[27] During the summer vacation of 1948 he recorded: "J and I paid one of our very rare visits to the cinema this afternoon to see Walt Disney's *Bambi*, the story of a deer, in which there were no human beings. Some beautiful autumnal colouring in the woods, and strokes of real genius here and there. Notably the prince of the deer, who, without caricature, was given a more than brutish dignity and majesty. Some good fooling, and some moments of great tenderness and terror."[28] If the Lewis brothers had lived into their eighties, they might have made one of their rare cinema visits to see *E. T.*, in which the characterization of the interplanetary visitor and the possibility of relationship between different rational species are reminiscent of Ransom's friendship with the Malacandrians (as is the poignant death scene).

The popularity of fantasy of all kinds must be one reason for Lewis's increasing fame. Undoubtedly another reason is the steadfastness of his Christian conviction in times of insecurity and rapid change. These two factors may—or may not (as Lewis might say)—be complementary. For some, fantasy provides merely an escape from the realities of this world. For those who understand Lewis (or, for instance, Tolkien, Charles Williams, Ursula LeGuin, or Madeleine L'Engle), fantasy offers imaginative models that may be more valid than our immediate perceptions of reality. Those who find no truth in fantasy may find no security in the works of C. S.

Lewis; he always alerted his readers to the false comforts of security, to the necessity of taking risks, and to the limitations of his own understanding.

In the Epilogue to *The Discarded Image,* Lewis developed the idea that our models, like the medieval Model of the Universe, are approximations that will be replaced by other models. He had acknowledged this human limitation throughout his writing; he indicated frequently that he knew he might be wrong, that he spoke according to his present understanding. In his first book, commenting on the earliest critics of Chaucer, he reminded his readers: "The stupidest contemporary, we may depend upon it, knew certain things about Chaucer's poetry which modern scholarship will never know; and doubtless the best of us misunderstand Chaucer in many places where the veriest fool among his audience could not have misunderstood."[29] Again, in summarizing Spenser's achievement, he began by saying: "If this chapter is not radically erroneous. . . ."[30] Such qualifications are so numerous in Lewis that the reader takes them for granted. "If I am not mistaken," "as far as I am concerned," "as it seems to me," and similar expressions remind us that he did not claim final authority on any matter of theory or opinion. The most apparently authoritarian of all his books, and hence the most controversial, *English Literature in the Sixteenth Century,* is full of verb phrases like "may have been," "could be considered," or "is arguable." At the beginning he stated his ignorance of the main feature of sixteenth-century literature: the relationship between the humanism of the *renascentia* and the flowering of Elizabethan poetry:

> . . . many móvements of thought which affected our literature would have been impossible without the recovery of Greek. But if there is any closer connexion than that

between the *renascentia* and the late sixteenth-century efflorescence of English literature, I must confess that it has escaped me. The more we look into the question, the harder we shall find it to believe that humanism had any power of encouraging, or any wish to encourage, the literature that actually arose. And it may be as well to confess immediately that I have no alternative "explanation" to offer. I do not claim to know why there were many men of genius at that time. The Elizabethans themselves would have attributed it to Constellation. I must be content with trying to sketch some of the intellectual and imaginative conditions under which they wrote.[31]

After 555 pages of such "sketching," Lewis came to an equally tentative conclusion:

When we look back on the sixteenth century our main impression must be one of narrow escapes and unexpected recoveries. . . . I do not suppose that the sixteenth century differs in these respects from any other arbitrarily selected stretch of years. It illustrates well enough the usual complex, unpatterned historical process; in which, while men often throw away irreplaceable wealth, they not infrequently escape what seemed inevitable dangers, not knowing that they have done either nor how they did it.[32]

Although Lewis's books were less erudite, much shorter, and much simpler in purpose and structure than his three major critical works, they were no less profound, and just as careful to avoid ultimata. His *Experiment in Criticism* was an attempt to define "good" literature in a new way; in the last chapter he did not claim to have discovered a rule by which it may be measured. "The nearest I have yet got to an answer is that we seek an enlargement of our being." The operative word here is *yet;* after a lifetime of reading and teaching, Lewis in his early sixties was still seeking to understand our reasons for "occupying our hearts with stories of what never happened and entering vicariously into feelings which we should try to avoid having in our own person."[33] The answer he had reached at that stage was powerfully appealing:

> We want to see with other eyes, to imagine with other imaginations, to feel with other hearts, as well as with our own. . . . we demand windows. Literature as Logos is a series of windows, even of doors.
>
> . . . In coming to understand anything we are rejecting the facts as they are for us in favour of the facts as they are.
>
> . . . this process can be described either as an enlargement or as a temporary annihilation of the self. But that is an old paradox; "he that loseth his life shall save it."[34]

Here again Lewis linked Platonism and Christianity. Literature as *Logos* is a window or a door for the reader whose focus is not on himself; yet his perspective is always his own, as Lewis cautioned: "so far as I can see."[35] Then he acknowledged the limits of his vision, seriously but not too solemnly: "Even the eyes of all humanity are not enough. I regret that the brutes cannot write books. Very gladly would I learn what face things present to a mouse or a bee; more gladly still would I perceive the olfactory world charged with all the information and emotion it carries for a dog."[36]

One of Lewis's clearest statements of his own limitations is in *The Four Loves.* Attempting to relate the first three human "loves" to Charity, the Love of God, more precisely than he had already done, he reminded the reader:

The precision can, of course, be only that of a model or a symbol, certain to fail us in the long run and even while we use it, requiring correction from other models. . . . We cannot see light, though by light we can see things. Statements about God are extrapolations from the knowledge of other things which the divine illumination enables us to know. . . . my efforts to be clear . . . may suggest a confidence which I by no means feel. I should be mad if I did. Take it as one man's reverie, almost one man's myth. If anything in it is useful to you, use it; if anything is not, never give it a second thought.[37]

Prefaced with this caveat, his model of Charity is concluded with equal caution. The last paragraph of the book begins "I dare not proceed. God knows, not I, whether I have ever tasted this love."[38] In fifteen lines there are three "if" clauses and "perhaps" occurs three times. When Lewis recorded *The Four Loves* as a series for American radio (The Episcopal Radio-TV Foundation, 1957), he laid down the script at the end and added, "Or so it seems to me." The producer deleted that qualification as possibly confusing to the radio audience for whom the talks were intended. Anyone familiar with Lewis's writing recognizes a characteristic attitude: his faith was unequivocal, but his knowledge, so much greater than most people's, seemed to him provisional. The windows, even the doors, may offer a view only "through a glass darkly."

Those who look to Lewis for final answers will be disappointed. Making no claims as a professional theologian or philosopher, he speculated in both fields as a believer and a thinker whose profession was the teaching of literature. In that role he offered models for consideration as possible and partial answers to the fundamental questions. To the seeker after truth he recommended risk rather than security. In his autobiographical narratives, the images were the antithesis of security: the early *Pilgrim's Regress* used stock allegory for his spiritual journey, with the irony that the direction was reversed; in the explicitly autobiographical *Surprised By Joy*, the title line from Wordsworth stresses the unexpected and inexplicable nature of spiritual experience. Responsiveness to the unexpected and willingness to take risks always take priority over security in Lewis's fiction. This was the element in Psyche's relationship with her husband that her sister could not understand. Orual demanded not only the security of power but the security of answers from the gods. Security, Lewis suggested in *Till We Have Faces*, is an illusion. This is why the Green Lady in *Perelandra* was forbidden to live on the Fixed Lands. Nor could the children remain in Narnia; each time they returned unexpectedly and by a different route. In *That Hideous Strength*, Mark's error was his desire for the security of a powerful institution, and Jane found that the peaceful old manor house offered her no refuge from disturbing dreams.

The choice of good over evil is always risky and often terrifying. Lewis expressed this idea clearly and powerfully in *The Lion, the Witch and the Wardrobe*:

" . . . Don't you know who is the King of Beasts? Aslan is a lion—*the* Lion, the great Lion."

"Ooh!" said Susan, "I'd thought he was a man. Is he quite safe? I shall feel rather nervous about meeting a lion."

"That you will, dearie, and no mistake," said Mrs. Beaver; "if there's anyone who can appear before Aslan without their knees knocking, they're either braver than most or else just silly."

"Then he isn't safe?" said Lucy.

"Safe?" said Mr. Beaver; "don't you hear what Mrs. Beaver tells you? Who said anything about safe? 'Course he isn't safe. But he's good. He's the King, I tell you."[39]

This conversation took place at the tea table in the Beavers' cozy home, just before they had to abandon it in order to evade the White Witch and find Aslan.

Lewis's emphasis on change and insecurity was expressed in a wide range of images, one of the most frequent of which was the open door. We yearn not merely to look out but to move out, like Tennyson's Ulysses, through the arch of experience to new worlds. This yearning explains, according to Lewis, the appeal of myth—the master key, which each can use to open the door of his choice. The key is used not to secure but to release. The same image appeared in a different context in Lewis's dedication of *A Preface to Paradise Lost* to Charles Williams: affirming his debt to Williams's lectures on Milton, he said his friend had "partly anticipated, partly confirmed, and most of all clarified and matured" his own views and had recovered a "true critical tradition after more than a hundred years of laborious misunderstanding."[40] Lewis evaluated Williams's achievement in terms of opening doors: "Apparently, the door of the prison was really unlocked all the time; but it was only you who thought of trying the handle. Now we can all come out."[41] While there is nothing original about the image of the open door, it is a clear example of one of Lewis's most basic premises. Perhaps it was no coincidence that we were standing at his open door when Lewis challenged me with the possibility of his writing something inconsistent with my conclusions.

He never did.

After my dissertation had been submitted, he published *Studies in Words, An Experiment in Criticism, A Grief*

Observed, and *The Discarded Image.* All of these books developed themes and ideas already suggested in earlier works. He was completely consistent.

What I wrote about Lewis more than twenty years ago was based, as is this book, on his literary career. I was not and still am not qualified to comment on his religious writing. From the viewpoint of a teacher of literature, I drew some conclusions about Lewis's significance that can now be tested by hindsight:

> What posterity's judgment of Lewis will be depends on the direction taken in the second half of the century not only by literature, but also by educational institutions and the church. Possibly his own image of himself as Old Western Man will determine his place in the history of our literature and literary criticism. But among his contemporaries he represents something more than a relic of the past. As the scope of knowledge expands and higher education increases, all academic fields become more and more highly specialized. This trend, which may be essential in nuclear physics, seems to Lewis disastrous in literature.
>
> His most important contribution is his attempt to preserve literary criticism as a normal human activity by attacking the barriers between research scholarship and spontaneous appreciation. Only as a distinguished scholar is he qualified to challenge the prerogatives of scholarship and defend the reader's supreme rights of enjoyment. In his opposition to sociological or psychoanalytical criticism, on the one hand, and diagrammatic or textual criticism, on the other, as ends in themselves, he steers a middle course which is never a mediocre or dull one. The vitality of his style and the paradoxical development of his arguments, whether challenging or exasperating, constitute what one critic has called "sublime pedagogy."[42]

Both his teaching and criticism are based on his confidence in the human imagination as a valid and ultimate criterion of literary merit, which provides an evaluation of the literature of the past and a corresponding direction for the literature of the future. His theory of *mythopoeia* could serve as the common denominator for criticism by both Christians and non-Christians of both Christian and non-Christian literature in the contemporary English literary world. His label of post-Christian for this society is a characteristic overstatement and partial truth. It is a semi-Christian society, and, one might add, a semiliterate society. Lewis's significance lies in his establishment of a meeting ground for all sides.

The admirer of Lewis is cautioned against making wider claims for him by a comment that he made about a statement of E. K. Chambers: "This seems . . . to be one of those rare propositions in literary history which are entirely true, and yet important."[43] The problem of making a generalization which is both true and important is particularly acute with a writer as versatile as Lewis. But it is possible to conclude that whatever reconciliation he effects between labor and delight, between Christian and pagan, or between past and present, will be all to the good.

These claims for Lewis were both too broad and too narrow. He has had less influence in England than I expected but far more in America. The importance of his literary theory has been overshadowed by the work of Northrop Frye and Joseph Campbell; the increasing interest in the nature and function of myth cannot be attributed to Lewis. His experiments with the novel form seem contrived and have never achieved the status of major works, whereas his children's stories are already classics. Lewis himself told the director of the

Episcopal Radio-TV Foundation that he would be remembered, if at all, for the *Chronicles of Narnia*. Perhaps he was right. Or perhaps he was trying to emphasize that he did not and his readers should not take him or his writing too seriously. He would not want to be idolized.

What C. S. Lewis represents for a wide range of readers is what he said we all look for in literature: an enlargement of our own limited experience. For many agnostics and skeptics, he has made faith intellectually acceptable and imaginatively appealing. For believers he has made exciting what had been taken for granted. In a period when change has been too rapid for some, even frightening for others, he has given us images of what is unchanging. He has guided us to perceive for ourselves the mythic patterns underlying our fluctuating reality. Lewis's emphasis on values of the old culture that we are in danger of losing need not be taken pessimistically. One of the most basic mythic patterns is that of loss and recovery; this movement may be slow and difficult to detect, but there are encouraging signs of recovery in our culture.

Three recent books about Lewis illustrate a new approach to his work that will make his basic message better understood. In *The Taste for the Other*, Gilbert Meilaender bases his analysis of Lewis's social and ethical thought on the doctrine of the "baptized imagination," the enjoyment of what is outside oneself, the "taste" for what is good in conduct that corresponds closely to the "taste" for what is good in literature. The importance of trusting the imagination is the core of Peter Schakel's *Reading With the Heart: The Way Into Narnia*; this fascinating study of the Narnia stories in terms of Northrop Frye's theory of archetypal structures demonstrates that the tales do not require this or any other academic criticism. The most encouraging sign of Lewis's potential influence is a book written by a young man while he was still in college: *C. S. Lewis and Scripture*, by Michael Christensen. The author addresses readers who, like himself, adhere to the doctrine of the inerrancy of the Scriptures. He shows in terms of Lewis's theory of mythopoeia that factual accuracy is not necessarily relevant to fundamental reality, that myth is not the opposite of truth but the embodiment of truth in forms accessible to the imagination. This book could help to reconcile the proponents of "Creation Science" in the classroom with their fellow Christians who make a distinction between science and poetry.

Other signs in our culture of recovery of what Lewis feared we might lose are too diverse to categorize, yet easy to observe. Doris Lessing's *Shikastra,* based on the Old Testament, the Torah, and the Apocrypha, represents a change of direction earlier indicated by her fantasy, *Memoirs of a Survivor.* Saul Bellow said at the end of *Humboldt's Gift* that his central character was going to Switzerland to study the philosophy of Rudolph Steiner (whose ideas were the subject of lifelong opposition between Lewis and Owen Barfield); his next novel, *The Dean's December,* evokes Dante in its concluding image of the stars. No one is surprised to see a unicorn on the cover of a high-school literary magazine. Fantasy is alive and well. But recovery of old values does not depend on preservation and repetition of old images. Lewis urged us to keep the door open. A professor from the Vanderbilt University School of Divinity wound up a weekend alumni seminar on the Bible by pointing out that the canon may not be closed yet. There are always possibilities of new revelation, as well as new discoveries in the caves of the Middle East or wherever. Readers of

C. S. Lewis, with their imaginations stimulated by his fiction and criticism, will be alert to recognize universal truth in new as well as old images. They will not limit their sights to any "beast slouching toward Bethlehem"; they will also be sensitive to the signs of "Aslan on the move."

NOTES

CHAPTER I

1. Chad Walsh, *C. S. Lewis: Apostle to the Skeptics* (New York: Macmillan, 1949).
2. C. S. Lewis, *De Descriptione Temporum* (Cambridge: Cambridge University Press, 1955), pp. 16–17.
3. Ibid., pp. 20–21.
4. C. S. Lewis, "Interim Report," *Cambridge Review*, April 21, 1956, p. 469.
5. C. S. Lewis, "Will We Lose God in Outer Space?" *Christian Herald*, 81 (April 1958), 19, 74–76.
6. "Faith and Outer Space," *Time*, 71 (March 31, 1958), 37.
7. Luther White, *The Image of Man in C. S. Lewis* (Nashville, Tenn.: Abingdon Press, 1969).
8. Joe R. Christopher and Joan K. Ostling, *C. S. Lewis: An Annotated Checklist of Writings About Him and His Works* (Kent, Ohio: Kent State University Press, 1974).

CHAPTER II

1. C. S. Lewis, *Letters of C. S. Lewis* (New York: Harcourt Brace, 1966), p. 163.
2. C. S. Lewis, "The Dethronement of Power," *Time and Tide*, 36 (October 22, 1955), 1374.
3. C. S. Lewis, *Rehabilitations and Other Essays* (London: Oxford University Press, 1939), p. 29.
4. C. S. Lewis, *God in the Dock*, ed. Walter Hooper (Grand Rapids, Mich.: Eerdmans, 1970).
5. C. S. Lewis, *The Allegory of Love* (Oxford: Oxford University Press, rpt. with corrections, 1938), passim, esp. p. 44.
6. C. S. Lewis, *English Literature in the Sixteenth Century, Excluding Drama* (Oxford: Oxford University Press, 1954), p. 4. (Referred to hereafter as *Sixteenth Century*.)

7. C. S. Lewis, *An Experiment in Criticism* (Cambridge: Cambridge University Press, 1961), p. 49.

8. C. S. Lewis, "Notes on the Way," *Time and Tide*, 27 (May 25, 1946), 485.

9. Lewis, *Sixteenth Century*, p. 17.

10. C. S. Lewis, "George Orwell," *Time and Tide*, 36 (January 8, 1955), 43.

11. Lewis, *The Allegory of Love*, p. 221.

12. C. S. Lewis, "The Gods Return to Earth," *Time and Tide*, 35 (August 14, 1954), 1082.

13. C. S. Lewis, Preface to *George MacDonald: An Anthology* (London: Geoffrey Bles, 1946), pp. 14–16.

14. C. S. Lewis, "Life Partners," *Time and Tide*, 31 (March 25, 1950), 286.

15. C. S. Lewis, "The Memory of Sir Walter Scott," in *The Edinburgh Sir Walter Scott Club Forty-ninth Annual Report* (Edinburgh, 1956), p. 18.

16. C. S. Lewis, "A Note on Jane Austen," *Essays in Criticism*, 4 (October 1954), 363.

17. Lewis, "George Orwell," pp. 43–44.

18. Lewis, *Sixteenth Century*, pp. 167ff.

19. C. S. Lewis, "Hamlet: The Prince or the Poem?" *Proceedings of the British Academy*, 28 (1942), 7–8.

20. Lewis, *Sixteenth Century*, p. 387.

21. C. S. Lewis, "Peace Proposals for Brother Every and Mr. Bethell," *Theology*, 41 (December 1940), 342.

22. Lewis, "The Gods Return to Earth," p. 1083.

23. Lewis, *Sixteenth Century*, pp. 379–80.

24. C. S. Lewis, "The Morte Darthur," review of *The Works of Sir Thomas Malory*, ed. E. Vinaver, in *Times Literary Supplement*, June 7, 1947, p. 274.

25. Lewis, "The Gods Return to Earth," p. 1083.

26. Lewis, *Rehabilitations*, p. 192.

27. Lewis, *The Allegory of Love*, p. 155.

28. Lewis, *Sixteenth Century*, p. 363.

29. Lewis, "Hamlet," p. 7.

30. C. S. Lewis, "Lilies That Fester," *Twentieth Century*, 157 (April 1955), 330–41.

31. Lewis, "Hamlet," p. 18.

32. C. S. Lewis, "Notes on the Way," *Time and Tide*, 27 (June 1, 1946), 510–11.

33. C. S. Lewis, "What Chaucer Really Did to *Il Filostrato*," *Essays and Studies by Members of the English Association*, 17 (1932), 56–75.

34. C. S. Lewis, "Is English Doomed?" *Spectator*, 172 (February 11, 1944), 121.

35. Lewis, *Rehabilitations*, p. 114.

36. C. S. Lewis, "Psycho-analysis and Literary Criticism," *Essays and Studies by Members of the English Association*, 27 (1942), 17.

37. C. S. Lewis and E. M. W. Tillyard, *The Personal Heresy* (London: Oxford University Press, 1939), passim.

38. Lewis, "Psycho-analysis and Literary Criticism," p. 7.

39. Lewis, *The Allegory of Love*, p. 194.

CHAPTER III

1. C. S. Lewis, *Surprised By Joy: The Shape of My Early Life* (New York: Harcourt, Brace and Company, 1955), pp. 199–200.

2. Lewis, *Letters*, p. 76.

3. Ibid., p. 217.

4. C. S. Lewis, *The Lion, the Witch and the Wardrobe* (London: Geoffrey Bles, 1950), p. 50.

5. Lewis, *The Allegory of Love*, p. viii.

6. Owen Barfield, *History in English Words* (London: Faber and Gwyer, 1926) and *Poetic Diction* (London: Faber and Gwyer, 1928).

7. Barfield, *Poetic Diction*, pp. 80–81.

8. Ibid., pp. 86–87.

9. C. S. Lewis, *Out of the Silent Planet* (London: The Bodley Head, 1938), pp. 152–53.

10. C. S. Lewis, *Perelandra* (London: The Bodley Head, 1943), p. 26.

11. Ibid., p. 67.

12. Ibid., p. 168.

13. C. S. Lewis, *That Hideous Strength* (London: The Bodley Head, 1945), pp. 280–81.

14. Ibid., p. 62.

15. Ibid., pp. 426–27.

16. Ibid., p. 338.

17. See the discussion of *Maya* in Owen Barfield, *Romanticism Comes of Age* (Middletown, Conn.: Wesleyan University Press, rpt. 1966), pp. 29–33.

18. C. S. Lewis, *Till We Have Faces: A Myth Retold* (New York: Harcourt, Brace and Company, 1956), p. 294.

19. C. S. Lewis, *The Voyage of the Dawn Treader* (London: Geoffrey Bles, 1952), p. 127.

20. Lewis, *The Lion, the Witch and the Wardrobe*, p. 129.

21. Ibid., p. 67.

22. Lewis, *The Voyage of the Dawn Treader,* pp. 142–43.

23. Lewis, *The Allegory of Love,* p. 1.

24. Ibid., p. 227.

25. Ibid., p. 49.

26. C. S. Lewis, *The Four Loves* (New York: Harcourt, Brace and Company, 1960), p. 53.

27. Ibid., pp. 170–71.

28. C. S. Lewis, *Studies in Words* (Cambridge: Cambridge University Press, 1960), p. 25.

29. Ibid., pp. 45–46.

30. Ibid., p. 74.

31. Ibid.

32. Ibid., p. 224.

33. Ibid., pp. 223–25.

34. Lewis, *The Allegory of Love,* pp. 312–13.

35. J. R. R. Tolkien, "On Fairy-Stories," in *Essays Presented to Charles Williams* (London: Oxford University Press, 1947), pp. 50–51.

36. C. S. Lewis, "Donne and Love Poetry in the Seventeenth Century," in *Seventeenth Century Studies Presented to Sir Herbert Grierson* (Oxford: Clarendon Press, 1938), pp. 72–73.

37. Lewis, *Sixteenth Century*, p. 148.

38. Lewis, *Letters,* p. 163.

CHAPTER IV

1. Kathleen Tillotson, review of *The Allegory of Love,* in *Review of English Studies,* 12 (October 1937), 477.

2. C. S. Lewis, *A Preface to Paradise Lost* (London: Oxford University Press, 1942), p. 139.

3. Lewis, *The Allegory of Love,* p. 1. Subsequent references to this work appear in the text.

4. C. S. Lewis, review of W. P. Ker, *Form and Style in Poetry,* ed. R. W. Chambers, in *The Oxford Magazine,* 47 (May 16, 1929), 284.

5. Lewis, *Sixteenth Century,* p. 1. Subsequent references to this work appear in the text.

6. Nevill Coghill, "The Approach to English" in *Light on C. S. Lewis,* ed. Jocelyn Gibb (New York: Harcourt Brace Jovanovich, 1976), p. 52.

7. Lewis, *Sixteenth Century,* p. 543.

8. Ibid., p. 541.

9. Ibid., p. 393.

10. Lewis, *A Preface to Paradise Lost,* p. 59.

11. Ibid., p. 64.

12. Ibid., p. 70.

13. Ibid., pp. 70–71.

14. Ibid., p. 129.

15. C. S. Lewis, "Christianity and Culture," *Theology,* 40 (March 1940), 170.

16. Lewis, *The Allegory of Love,* pp. 75–76.

17. The importance of this longing or *Sehnsucht* is developed fully in Corbin Carnell, *Bright Shadow of Reality* (Grand Rapids, Mich.: Eerdmans, 1974). This sensitive study of a major theme in Lewis's work is the best analysis I have read of the relationship between his literary criticism and his Christian apologetics.

18. Lewis, *A Preface to Paradise Lost,* p. 90.

19. C. S. Lewis, lecture on Milton's minor poems, Oxford University, November 25, 1955.

20. Lewis, *Sixteenth Century*, p. 328.

21. Lewis, "The Memory of Sir Walter Scott," p. 19.

22. Lewis, *The Allegory of Love*, p. 210.

23. C. S. Lewis, *Mere Christianity* (London: Fontana, 1952), p. 6.

CHAPTER V

1. Coghill, "The Approach to English," p. 65.

2. C. S. Lewis, *They Asked For a Paper: Papers and Addresses* (London: Geoffrey Bles, 1962).

3. Coghill, p. 65.

4. Lewis, *Studies in Words*, pp. 218–19.

5. Lewis, *Letters*, p. 271.

6. Ibid., pp. 291–92.

7. John Lawlor, "The Tutor and the Scholar," in *Light on C. S. Lewis*, ed. Jocelyn Gibb, pp. 68–77.

8. Ibid., p. 73.

9. Humphrey Carpenter, *The Inklings* (New York: Houghton Mifflin, 1979), p. 58.

10. Ibid., p. 214.

11. Derek Brewer, "The Tutor: A Portrait," in *C. S. Lewis at the Breakfast Table*, ed. J. T. Como (New York: Macmillan, 1979), p. 43.

12. Ibid., p. 76.

13. John Wain, "C. S. Lewis," *The American Scholar*, 50:1 (Winter 1980–81), 80.

14. Roger Lancelyn Green and Walter Hooper, *C. S. Lewis: A Biography* (New York: Harcourt Brace Jovanovich, 1974), p. 140.

15. Kathleen Raine, "From a Poet," in *Light on C. S. Lewis*, ed. Jocelyn Gibb, p. 103.

16. Lewis, *Surprised By Joy*, p. 112.

17. Ibid., p. 136.

18. Ibid., p. 112.

19. Quoted from a letter to M. L. Charlesworth, April 9, 1940.

20. Lewis, *That Hideous Strength*, p. 291.

21. Ibid., pp. 266–74.

22. Ibid., pp. 279–81.

23. Ibid., pp. 457-62.

24. Lewis, *The Lion, the Witch and the Wardrobe*, pp. 49–50.

25. Ibid., pp. 50–51.

26. Ibid., pp. 172–73.

27. Lewis, *Till We Have Faces*, pp. 6–7. Subsequent references to this work appear in the text.

28. Lewis, *That Hideous Strength*, pp. 159–61.

29. C. S. Lewis, *The Abolition of Man* (New York: Macmillan, rpt. 1955), p. 55.

30. Lewis, *The Voyage of the Dawn Treader*, p. 9.

31. Ibid., p. 83.

32. Lewis, *An Experiment in Criticism*, p. 8.

33. Ibid., p. 89.

34. Ibid.

35. Ibid., p. 91.

36. Ibid., p. 1.

37. Lewis, *Rehabilitations*, pp. 95–116.

38. Lewis, *Sixteenth Century*, p. 314.

39. Lewis, *An Experiment in Criticism*, p. 92.

40. Ibid., pp. 92–94.

41. Ibid., p. 132.

42. Ibid., pp. 136–37.

43. Ibid., pp. 140–41.

CHAPTER VI

1. C. S. Lewis, "Interim Report," *Cambridge Review*, April 21, 1956, p. 468.

2. Lewis, *A Preface to Paradise Lost*, p. 1.

3. Lewis, *The Allegory of Love*, p. 1.

4. C. S. Lewis, *The Discarded Image* (Cambridge: Cambridge University Press, 1964), p. vii.

5. Ibid., pp. vii–viii.

6. Lewis, *The Allegory of Love*, p. 7.

7. Lewis, *Sixteenth Century*, p. 79.

8. Lewis, *The Allegory of Love*, p. 190.

9. C. S. Lewis, "Kipling's World," in *Literature and Life: Addresses to the English Association,* I (London: Harrap and Co., 1948), 58–59.

10. Ibid., pp. 57–58.

11. Lewis, *Surprised by Joy*, p. 136.

12. Lewis, *Sixteenth Century*, p. 336.

13. Ibid., p. 302.

14. Ibid., pp. 557–58.

15. Lewis, *A Preface to Paradise Lost*, p. 20.

16. Lewis, *Rehabilitations*, pp. 95–116 passim.

17. Lewis, *An Experiment in Criticism*, pp. 2–3.

18. Ibid., p. 33.

19. Lewis, *Sixteenth Century*, pp. 64–65.

20. Ibid., p. 478.

21. Ibid., p. 481.

22. Ibid.

23. Ibid., p. 482.

24. Lewis, "The Memory of Sir Walter Scott," p. 18.

25. Typescript in the files of the Edinburgh Sir Walter Scott Club.

26. Lewis, *Sixteenth Century*, p. 462.

27. Lewis, *A Preface to Paradise Lost,* pp. 79–80.

28. Lewis, *The Allegory of Love*, p. 65.

29. Lewis, *A Preface to Paradise Lost*, p. 70.

30. Lewis, *Sixteenth Century*, p. 371.

31. Ibid., p. 400.

32. Ibid., p. 529.

33. Lewis, "Donne and Love Poetry in the Seventeenth Century," p. 65.

34. Lewis, *Sixteenth Century*, p. 360.

35. Ibid., p. 498.

36. Lewis, *A Preface to Paradise Lost*, pp. 59–60.

37. Lewis, *Sixteenth Century*, p. 240.
38. Lewis, *A Preface to Paradise Lost,* pp. 10–11.
39. Ibid., p. 2.
40. Ibid., p. 83.
41. Ibid., pp. 131–32.
42. Ibid., pp. 132–33.

CHAPTER VII

1. C. S. Lewis, *Arthurian Torso* (London: Oxford University Press, 1948), p. 187.
2. Lewis, *Sixteenth Century*, p. 275.
3. C. V. Wedgwood, *The Sense of the Past* (Cambridge: Cambridge University Press, 1957), p. 14.
4. Lewis, *Sixteenth Century*, p. 393.
5. Lewis, *The Allegory of Love*, p. 360.
6. Lewis, *Sixteenth Century*, pp. 392–93.
7. C. S. Lewis, *On Stories and Other Essays On Literature,* ed. Walter Hooper (New York: Harcourt Brace Jovanovich, 1982), p. 21.
8. Lewis, *Arthurian Torso*, p. 96.
9. Roger Lancelyn Green, "Logres," *Oxford Magazine,* November 18, 1948, p. 161.
10. Lewis, *The Discarded Image*, p. 222.
11. Ibid., p. 14.
12. Lewis, *Letters,* p. 217.
13. Ibid., p. 267.
14. Ibid., p. 271.
15. Lewis, *The Lion, the Witch and the Wardrobe*, p. 19.
16. Lewis, *Out of the Silent Planet*, p. 62.
17. C. S. Lewis, *The Great Divorce* (London: Geoffrey Bles, 1945), p. vii.
18. Ibid., p. viii.
19. C. S. Lewis, *The Magician's Nephew* (London: The Bodley Head, 1955), chap. ix.

20. C. S. Lewis, *The Last Battle* (London: The Bodley Head, 1956), p. 166.

21. Ibid., p. 167.

22. Ibid., pp. 170–71.

23. Lewis, *Perelandra*, pp. 228–30.

24. Lewis, *On Stories and Other Essays*, p. 5.

25. C. S. Lewis, *They Stand Together: The Letters of C. S. Lewis to Arthur Greeves (1914–1963)* (New York: Macmillan, 1979), p. 46.

26. Warren H. Lewis, *Brothers and Friends*, ed. Clyde S. Kilby and Marjorie Lamp Mead (San Francisco: Harper & Row, 1982), p. 116.

27. Ibid., p. 175.

28. Ibid., p. 221.

29. Lewis, *The Allegory of Love*, p. 163.

30. Ibid., p. 357.

31. Lewis, *Sixteenth Century*, p. 2.

32. Ibid., pp. 557–58.

33. Lewis, *An Experiment in Criticism*, p. 137.

34. Ibid., pp. 137–38.

35. Ibid., p. 139.

36. Ibid., p. 140.

37. Lewis, *The Four Loves*, pp. 174–75.

38. Ibid., p. 192.

39. Lewis, *The Lion, the Witch and the Wardrobe*, p. 77.

40. Lewis, *A Preface to Paradise Lost*, p. v.

41. Ibid., p. vi.

42. Ralph Maud, "C. S. Lewis's Inaugural," *Essays in Criticism*, 5:4 (October 1955), 392.

43. C. S. Lewis, review of *Sir Thomas Wyatt and Some Collected Studies*, ed. E. K. Chambers, in *Medium Aevum*, 3:3 (October 1934), 240.

SELECTED BIBLIOGRAPHY

PRIMARY SOURCES: BOOKS BY C. S. LEWIS

The Abolition of Man, or, Reflections on Education with Special Reference to the Teaching of English in the Upper Forms of Schools. (Riddell Memorial Lectures, Fifteenth Series.) New York: Macmillan, rpt. 1955.

The Allegory of Love: A Study in Medieval Tradition. Oxford: Oxford University Press, rpt. with corrections, 1938.

Arthurian Torso: Containing the Posthumous Fragment of 'The Figure of Arthur' by Charles Williams and a Commentary on the Arthurian Poems of Charles Williams by C. S. Lewis. London: Oxford University Press, 1948.

De Descriptione Temporum. Cambridge: Cambridge University Press, 1955.

The Discarded Image: An Introduction to Medieval and Renaissance Literature. Cambridge: Cambridge University Press, 1964.

English Literature in the Sixteenth Century, Excluding Drama. (The Oxford History of English Literature, Vol. III.) Oxford: Oxford University Press, 1954.

An Experiment in Criticism. Cambridge: Cambridge University Press, 1961.

The Four Loves. New York: Harcourt, Brace and Company, 1960.

The Horse and His Boy. London: Geoffrey Bles, 1954.

The Last Battle: A Story for Children. London: The Bodley Head, 1956.

Letters of C. S. Lewis. Ed. W. H. Lewis. New York: Harcourt Brace, 1966.

The Lion, the Witch and the Wardrobe: A Story for Children. London: Geoffrey Bles, 1950.

The Magician's Nephew. London: The Bodley Head, 1955.

On Stories and Other Essays on Literature. Ed. Walter Hooper. New York: Harcourt Brace Jovanovich, 1982.

Out of the Silent Planet. London: The Bodley Head, 1938.

Perelandra. London: The Bodley Head, 1943.

A Preface to Paradise Lost: Being the Ballard Matthews Lectures Delivered at University College, North Wales, 1941, Revised and Enlarged. London: Oxford University Press, 1942.

Prince Caspian: The Return to Narnia. London: Geoffrey Bles, 1951.

Rehabilitations and Other Essays. London: Oxford University Press, 1939.

The Silver Chair. London: Geoffrey Bles, 1953.

Studies in Words. Cambridge: Cambridge University Press, 1960.

Surprised By Joy: The Shape of My Early Life. New York: Harcourt, Brace and Company, 1955.

That Hideous Strength: A Modern Fairy-Tale for Grown-ups. London: The Bodley Head, 1945.

They Asked For a Paper: Papers and Addresses. London: Geoffrey Bles, 1962.

Till We Have Faces: A Myth Retold. New York: Harcourt, Brace and Company, 1956.

The Voyage of the Dawn Treader. London: Geoffrey Bles, 1952.

SECONDARY SOURCES

Barfield, Owen. *History in English Words.* London: Faber and Gwyer, 1926.

———. *Poetic Diction.* London: Faber and Gwyer, 1928.

Carnell, Corbin. *Bright Shadow of Reality.* Grand Rapids, Mich.: Eerdmans, 1974.

Christensen, Michael. *C. S. Lewis on Scripture.* Waco, Tex.: Word Books, 1979.

Christopher, Joe R., and Joan K. Ostling. *C. S. Lewis: An Annotated Checklist of Writings About Him and His Works.* Kent, Ohio: Kent State University Press, 1974.

Como, James T. (ed.). *C. S. Lewis at the Breakfast Table.* New York: Macmillan, 1979.

Gibb, Jocelyn (ed.). *Light on C. S. Lewis.* New York: Harcourt Brace Jovanovich, 1976.

Glover, Donald E. *C. S. Lewis: The Art of Enchantment.* Athens, Ohio: Ohio University Press, 1981.

Green, Roger Lancelyn, and Walter Hooper. *C. S. Lewis: A Biography.* New York: Harcourt Brace Jovanovich, 1974.

Kilby, Clyde. *The Christian World of C. S. Lewis.* Grand Rapids, Mich.: Eerdmans, 1964.

Lewis, Warren H. *Brothers and Friends: The Diaries of Major Warren Hamilton Lewis,* ed. Clyde S. Kilby and Marjorie Lamp Mead. San Francisco: Harper & Row, 1982.

Meilaender, Gilbert. *The Taste for the Other: The Social and Ethical Thought of C. S. Lewis.* Grand Rapids, Mich.: Eerdmans, 1978.

Schakel, Peter. *Reading With the Heart: The Way Into Narnia.* Grand Rapids, Mich.: Eerdmans, 1979.

INDEX